April 19, 1775:
A Historiographical Study

Douglas P. Sabin

CONTENTS

AUTHOR'S INTRODUCTION

This study was written to provide Minute Man National Historical Park's interpreters with an objective and accurate information source to aid them in the interpretation of the park's major theme, the battle which occurred on April 19, 1775. It may also serve as a historical database for any proposed park exhibit showing the movement of troops in the first clash of arms between the organized American militia and the Regular British Army.

Prior to the start of this study, it was felt that many of the existing published secondary sources on April 19, 1775, were either incomplete in the coverage of events, inaccurate in certain details, or too subjective due to the bias of earlier local writers. In researching this historiographical study, therefore, the author drew heavily from published primary source material. Before conclusions were reached, the author, whenever possible, consulted the eyewitness accounts of battle participants or those who witnessed the fighting. In cases where eyewitness accounts conflicted, the author has stated both sides so that the reader is aware of the controversy surrounding certain historical details.

At this point a few comments concerning the credibility of the major primary sources are in order. Excluding the subjective American newspaper accounts of the battle, the prime published sources of eyewitness accounts to the Battle of April 19, 1775, are the original depositions by battle participants. These were sworn to on April 23, 24, and 25, 1775, by the direction of the Second Provincial Congress. These consisted of 21 separate documents which were carried to England soon after the battle by Captain John Derby of Salem. The purpose of these depositions was to prove that the British were the aggressors on April 19, 1775, and to gain sympathy for Massachusetts both in England and America.

The 21 original depositions were soon printed along with an account of the fighting entitled <u>A Narrative of the Excursion of General Gage, on the Nineteenth of April 1775: Together with</u>

the Depositions Taken by Order of the Congress, to Support the Truth of It. Printed by the authority of Massachusetts Bay, this publication is the official account of the Second Provincial Congress. The Narrative and the 21 original depositions are suspect as objective historical documents. They were written primarily for propaganda purposes in support of the Massachusetts contention that the British were to blame for the bloodshed on April 19, 1775.

In 1825, some 50 years after the event, later sworn depositions were taken from ten surviving witnesses or battle participants. These aged men were all from Lexington. The purpose of their depositions was to refute a claim that the first active resistance to the British occurred at Concord and not Lexington. These later Lexington depositions were first printed in Elias Phinney's History of the Battle of Lexington, published in 1825. Mr. Phinney and others in Lexington greatly resented the passive role some historians had assigned to the Lexington Militia Company on the morning of April 19, 1775. The purpose of the 1825 Lexington depositions was to prove that the Lexington Militia Company did actively resist the British on Lexington Common. In evaluating the objectivity of the later Lexington depositions, one must keep in mind the purpose for which they were written, the age of the men making the sworn statements, and the fifty years that had passed since the events in question.

In 1827, in response to Lexington's claims, four new sworn depositions were taken in support of the Concord position that the Lexington Militia Company did not fire back on Lexington Common. These 1827 depositions were printed in the publication A History of the Fight at Concord on the 19th of April 1775. This little publication was written by Ezra Ripley of Concord. Again, the purpose for which these depositions were taken and the time and age factors must be considered in determining their historical worth.

Following the publication of Lemuel Shattuck's History of Concord in 1835, Acton native Josiah Adams was greatly disturbed by Mr. Shattuck's remarks concerning the role of

Captain Isaac Davis and his Acton Minute Company. Mr. Adams thought that Lemuel Shattuck had treated Davis unfairly and had exaggerated the role played by the Concord Companies on April 19, 1775. In response to Mr. Shattuck, Josiah Adams published six new depositions by Acton citizens in support of the Acton position relating to the action on April 19, 1775.

The feud between Concord and Acton raged for years and on April 22, 1850, Josiah Adams took the sworn statement of Amos Baker, the last known survivor of the fight at the North Bridge.

The original 21 depositions taken within a week of the battle to support the Massachusetts position that the British were the aggressors on April 19, 1775, and the later depositions taken from aged men against the background of inter-town feuding are far from objective historical documents. Nevertheless, if read carefully and compared against other evidence, these American early and later depositions are prime historical resource material.

It should be noted that other depositions were taken that are of interest to the historian. These mainly concern the payment of claims for property losses on April 19, 1775. They often contain details relating to the activities that occurred on April 19, 1775.

The account of Paul Revere and his famous ride, as described by Revere himself, is another important primary source relating to the events of April 19, 1775. Revere's account has been published in several sources which are easily available to the historian.

Other revealing American primary sources related to April 19, 1775, include letters by Thaddeus Blood, Amos Barrett, and the Rev. Edmund Foster. Captain Gideon Foster's account is also interesting as is the diary account of Rev. William Emerson. Major-General William Heath's memoirs are also informative, although they give fewer details than one might expect from the ranking American officer in the field on April 19, 1775.

The British primary accounts are of equal importance to the student of the Battle of April 19, 1775. These include letters, reports, and journals written by the officers who participated in the military operation on April 19, 1775. Of prime importance are General Gage's orders to Lt. Col. Frances Smith and Col.

Smith's report to General Gage concerning his mission to Concord. Of equal, if not more importance, are the reports of Brigadier-General Hugh Earl Percy, Major John Pitcairn, Captain Walter S. Laurie, Lt. William Sutherland, and Ensign DeBerniere to General Gage, relating to the action on April 19, 1775. General Gage's official report of the operation on April 19, 1775, to his superior in England is disappointing in its brevity.

Also of large importance to the official reports and letters written within the British military are the unofficial British correspondence and diary accounts. As these may be less shaded than the official reports, they should be studied carefully by the student of April 19, 1775. These include the diary accounts of Lt. Frederick Mackenzie and Lt. John Barker, the narrative account of Ensign Jeremy Lister, and the letter of Lt. Col. Frances Smith to his friend R. Donkin. The informal correspondence of Lord Percy to his father and others prior to April 19, 1775, should also be read as they reflect Percy's attitude and impressions prior to the outbreak of fighting.

Of the secondary sources that have been published, there is no one account of the entire Battle of April 19, 1775, that tells the complete story in adequate detail. Perhaps the best secondary account is The Day of Concord and Lexington by the Concord historian, Allen French. Published in 1925, Mr. French's book is thin on detail concerning the British return march east of Meriam's Corner. The author was also unaware of Major Pitcairn's report to General Gage concerning the events on Lexington Common at the time he wrote The Day of Concord and Lexington. He later corrected his omission in his later book entitled General Gage's Informers, which should be read as a sequel to his earlier book.

Other leading secondary works on the Battle of April 19, 1775, include Frank Warren Coburn's The Battle of April 19, 1775 and John R. Galvin's The Minute Men. Mr. Coburn's book, published in 1912, provides more detail of the fighting during the British return march to Boston than most books, but it contains some inaccurate statements and doubtful interpretations. It will always be consulted, however, as it contains a listing of the American battle participants taken from the muster rolls of April 19, 1775. While Mr. Galvin's book contains some imaginative interpretations, much of the detail he provides is not supported by the sources he has cited.

There are a few shorter works of worth including Harold Murdock's <u>The Nineteenth of April 1775</u> and Arthur B. Tourtellot's <u>Lexington and Concord</u>, but their coverage of the entire battle is too thin. What has always been lacking in the historical accounts of the Battle of April 19, 1775, is an objective detailed account of the entire battle. Too often, the historical works related to the battle have been either too brief or were written by amateur historians from a local point of view. Hopefully, the account contained in this historiographical study will provide a more complete and objective view of the entire battle which opened the Revolutionary War.

In researching this study the author owes a debt of gratitude to the professional and many amateur historians, whose works he consulted over the years. Perhaps the strongest words of appreciation should go to those actual battle participants, both American and British, who took the time to record their recollections of the battle whose thunder echoes around the world. I should also thank Superintendent Robert Nash and Chief of Interpretation Fred Szarka of Minute Man National Historical Park, whose support over the years I worked on the project were essential to its ultimate conclusion. Last, but by no means least, I would like to acknowledge Darlene Besso for the countless hours she has spent in processing my drafts of this study.

-Douglas P. Sabin
September 17, 1987

1 - THE BRITISH ARE COMING

By the spring of 1775, the Province of Massachusetts was in a virtual state of rebellion. Patriot leaders had established a Provincial Congress, which had assumed two of the most important prerogatives of government: the tax gathering function and control of the Province's militia force.

In lieu of paying their taxes to the established Crown Government, the people of the Province of Massachusetts Bay allowed agents recently appointed by the Provincial Congress to collect their taxes. The money raised was used to finance a citizen militia force, which was independent of Crown control. Indeed, Governor-General Thomas Gage, from his Boston headquarters, feared that this militia force would be used to drive his small professional army out of Boston.

Following the passage of the so-called Coercive Acts in 1774, the British Army in Boston had been reinforced by the arrival of new regiments. General Gage, however, could have had no more than 4,000 troops under his direct control in Boston. In addition to these soldiers, Gage was supported by vessels of the British Navy under Vice Admiral Samuel Graves. With these forces at his disposal, Gage was able to control the port city of Boston, its harbor, and offshore waters. He could also influence such towns as Charlestown, which was under the guns of the ships moored in the nearby waters. He had no control, however, over the country outside of Boston, as the leaders of the militia were loyal to the Province and were out of Gage's control.

During the winter of 1774 and 1775, General Gage had ordered a number of marches outside of Boston. These marches served a dual purpose. They not only gave the men much needed exercise, but they kept the colonials off guard as to British intentions. On several occasions, armed militia units had appeared within sight of Gage's troops, but a clash between the British and the militia had thus far been avoided.

The Massachusetts Militia establishment had, in fact, been purged and reorganized. In the preceding fall of 1774, the Patriot leaders forced resignations from all militia officers including those loyal to the Crown. The officers who were elected in their place felt that they owed their loyalty to the Province and not Governor-General Thomas Gage or the established Royal government.

On October 26, 1774, a committee of the First Provincial Congress meeting in Concord submitted a report, upon which a resolve was quickly passed. This resolve provided for the appointment of a Committee of Safety, whose members were empowered to arm and assemble as many of the militia as necessary for the protection and defense of the inhabitants of Massachusetts and their property. In Massachusetts at that time, almost every able-bodied white male citizen between the ages of sixteen and sixty was a member of the militia.

The Committee of the First Provincial Congress also resolved that companies that had not chosen officers should do so immediately, and that these elected company officers should then meet and choose their field officers. General officers would be appointed by the authority of the First Provincial Congress. As the rank and file of the Massachusetts militia were pro-Whig and anti-Tory, these elections resulted in the removal of any officer suspected of still harboring strong loyalties to the Royal Government.

The new field officers were further directed to enlist at least one quarter of the militia companies and form companies of 50 privates, who were to equip and hold themselves in readiness to march upon the shortest notice from the Committee of Safety. Each of these companies was ordered to choose a captain and two lieutenants to command them. These elected officers were then directed to form their instant response companies into battalions to consist of nine companies each, and that the officers within the companies of the newly formed battalions proceed to elect field officers to command them. The resolve of the First Provincial Congress further directed that if the members of this force lacked arms and ammunition, the selectmen of the towns were responsible for equipping its men as provided by law.[1]

The October 26, 1774, resolve thus created the instant response mobile forces, which became known as minute men to distinguish them from the larger body of the established militia from which they were created.

In February of 1775, The Provincial Congress ordered that sufficient military arms and provisions to furnish 15,000 men be collected and stored at Concord and Worcester. In addition to food supplies such as pork, fish, and flour, these supplies included musket balls and both brass and iron cannon. The military stores in Concord were under the charge of Colonel James Barrett of Concord, who was directed on March 15 by the Committee of Safety to obtain a sufficient number of faithful men to maintain a constant nightly guard over the stores. Colonel Barrett was also instructed to maintain enough teams on hand to move the stores on short notice to safer locations.[2]

General Thomas Gage was very much aware that military supplies were stored at Concord and Worcester. In addition to his paid informers, Gage also gained intelligence from Loyalists scattered throughout the Province. He also sent out soldiers

---

[1] Norman Castle, Editor, The Minute Men, Yankee Colour Corporation, Southborough, Massachusetts, 1977, p. VIII.

[2] Lemuel Shattuck, A History of the Town of Concord, Russell, Odiorne and Company, Concord, 1835, p. 95.

disguised as civilians to sketch maps of the roads and other terrain features that might have relevance to military operations in the country outside of Boston. Two such spies were Captain Brown of the 52nd Regiment and Ensign DeBerniere of the 10th Regiment. The two officers visited Worcester in February and on March 20, 1775, they journeyed to Concord after passing through Weston and Sudbury. According to DeBerniere's narrative journal, they stayed at the home of the Concord Tory, Daniel Bliss.

Gage was disturbed by the growing supply of military arms and supplies at Concord and Worcester. He was also under political pressure to take some effective action to snap the rebellious province back into line. There were many Tory supporters in both England and America who felt that what was needed was a strong show of British force and that the Americans would quickly give in. In his letter to Lord Sandwich on March 4, 1775, Major John Pitcairn of the Royal Marines wrote in part:

"I am satisfied that one active campaign, a smart action, and burning two or three of their towns, will set everything to rights. Nothing now, I am afraid, but this will ever convince those foolish bad people that England is in earnest."[3]

On what day Gage decided to send troops to Concord is unknown. As early as April 5, he had written to Vice Admiral Graves asking the Admiral how many troops his boats in the harbor could take aboard.[4] Graves sought a meeting with Gage

---

[3] William Bell Clark, Editor, Naval Documents of the American Revolution, Vol. I (letter dated March 4, 1775, from Major John Pitcairn to Lord Sandwich), Superintendent of Documents, Washington, D. C., 1964, p. 125.

[4] Ibid. (letter dated April 5, 1775, from General Thomas Gage to Vice Admiral Samuel Graves), pp. 168-169.

the next day at 10 a.m., and it is not unlikely that the two officers discussed a future expedition to Concord.[5]

It should be noted that the colonials had set up an organization to keep the British under observation. Paul Revere wrote:

"In the fall of 1774 and winter of 1775, I was one of upwards of thirty, chiefly mechanics who formed ourselves into a committee for the purpose of watching the movements of the British soldiers and gaining every intelligence of the movements of the Tories."[6]

On April 16, about midnight, Paul Revere observed that the boats the British had previously repaired were launched and "carried under the sterns of the men of war."[7] The day before, the alert colonials had noted that the grenadiers and light infantry were taken off their regular duties for "exercise and new evolutions."[8]

Normally, each British regiment in Boston had a light infantry company and grenadier company assigned to it. The information concerning the removal of these troops, the British "flank" companies, from their normal duties, combined with the intelligence that the British had repaired their boats and were maintaining them in a state of readiness, had been reported to the Committee of Safety. The Committee suspected that the British were planning a raid on the military supplies stored at Concord.

General Gage had indeed decided to destroy the military supplies at Concord. He realized that if his mission was to

---

[5] Ibid. (letter dated April 5, 1775, from Vice Admiral Samuel Graves to General Thomas Gage), pp. 168-169.

[6] Edward Field, The Colonial Tavern, Preston and Rounds, Providence, 1897, p. 260.

[7] Boston National Historic Sites Commission to the Congress of the United States, Interim Report, The Lexington-Concord Battle Road, 1958, p. 47.

[8] Ibid.

succeed he had to have the element of surprise. Therefore, hoping that darkness would mask his troops' movements, Gage ordered Lieutenant Colonel Francis Smith to march to Concord on the evening of April 18 and 19 with the grenadier and light infantry companies. According to Gage's written orders dated April 18, 1775, Smith was "to seize and destroy all artillery, ammunition, provisions, tents, small arms and military stores."[9] Smith's orders also cautioned him against plundering the inhabitants or damaging private property.

Gage hoped to keep the destination of his troops a secret so he didn't tell his men where they were going. About ten o'clock on the evening of April 18, the grenadiers and light infantry were awakened by the touch and soft whispers of their sergeants. They were then conducted out of the barracks by a back way without the knowledge of the other soldiers or the sentries.[10]

Marching silently in small parties to the Charles River, the soldiers found a number of the Navy's boats in waiting. The soldiers were rowed across the river to the Cambridge side where they were landed at Phipp's Farm. The boats then returned to the Boston shore for the remaining troops, and it was not until two o'clock or so in the morning that the British finally started their march to Concord.

Lieutenant John Barker of the Fourth Regiment of Foot, better known as the King's Own, left us with the following diary account after the British had crossed the Charles.

"After getting over the marsh where we were wet up to our knees, we were halted in a dirty road and stood there 'till two oclock in the morning waiting for provisions to be brought from the boats and to be devided, and which most of the men threw away, having carried some with 'em. At two

---

[9] Concord Chamber of Commerce, The Lexington-Concord Battle Road, p. 3.

[10] Interim Report, p. 51.

oclock we began our march by wading through a very long ford up to our middles."[11]

Frank W. Coburn, writing in 1912, believed the ford Lt. Barker mentioned in his diary was Willis Creek. According to Coburn, the British were forced to wade the creek as Lt. Col. Smith thought that the soldiers would make too much noise in marching over the nearby Bullard's Bridge.[12]

It should be noted that the two trips the boats had to make, combined with the added time lost in dividing the apparently unneeded provisions and wading Willis Creek, gave the Colonials additional time to prepare for the British expedition to Concord. It would have saved the British much time had they been able to transport all their men and supplies across in one trip on the boats.

According to Lieutenant Frederick Mackenzie, the Adjutant of the Royal Welch Fusiliers, Lt. Col. Francis Smith and his second in command, Major John Pitcairn, had the following companies with them when they embarked on the river crossing:

Grenadiers--4th, 5th, 10th, 18th, 23rd, 38th, 43rd, 47th, 59th, 1st and 2nd Marines.

Light Infantry--4th, 5th, 10th, 23rd, 38th, 43rd, 47th, 59th, 1st and 2nd Marines.[13]

---

[11] Elizabeth Ellery Dana, Editor, The British in Boston: Being the Diary of Lieutenant John Barker of the King's Own Regiment from November 15, 1774 to May 31, 1776, Harvard University Press, Cambridge, 1924, pp. 31-32.

[12] Frank Warren Coburn, The Battle of April 19, 1775, in Lexington, Concord, Lincoln, Arlington, Cambridge, Somerville and Charlestown, Massachusetts, F. L. Coburn & Co., Boston, 1912, p. 47.

[13] Allen French, Editor, A British Fusilier in Revolutionary Boston: Being the Diary of Lieutenant Frederick Mackenzie, Adjutant of the Royal Welch Fusiliers, January 5 - April 30, 1775, Harvard University Press, Cambridge, 1926, p. 51.

DOUGLAS P. SABIN

The late historian Allen French believed that Lt. Mackenzie was in error when he included the Second Battalion of Marines on the list. French also believed Mackenzie was mistaken when he omitted the two companies from the 52nd Regiment, as the casualties of the 52nd included a sergeant and five privates.[14]

French is supported in his belief that the 52nd marched with Smith by the fact that Private John Bateman of the 52nd Regiment left a deposition dated April 23, 1775, stating that the British fired on the men gathered near the meeting-house.[15] This deposition, from the captured British soldier, of course, refers to the fighting on Lexington Common which Bateman witnessed.

If Mackenzie was wrong by including the Second Battalion of Marines with Smith, and if French was right in his addition of the 52nd to Smith's companies, it would appear that Smith marched with 21 companies under his command. Twenty-one companies is the consensus figure given by the various authors concerned with the subject.

Allen French also cited 32 as the average number of men in each British company. Apparently, he based this average on Lt. Mackenzie's statement that two companies of the Fusiliers contained 64 men. Harold Murdock also gave 32 as an average. If French and Murdock were right on this average, the British force under Smith contained about 672 men if 21 companies came with him. If 23 companies came out, Smith's force would have consisted of 736 or so men according to French. For years the interpreters at Minute Man National Historical Park have used "about 700" as the number of men under Lt. Col. Francis Smith's command. "About 700" is probably not far from the historic reality of the situation.

According to Lt. John Barker, Smith's force marched only a few miles before they captured "three of four people who were going off to give intelligence."[16] Frank W. Coburn believed that

---

[14] Ibid., pp. 51-52.

[15] Clement C. Sawtell, Editor, The Nineteenth of April 1775: A Collection of First Hand Accounts, "Deposition of John Bateman, April 23, 1775," p. 671.

[16] Dana, "Diary of Lt. John Barker," p. 32.

the first two men captured were Thomas Robins and David Harrington of Lexington. According to Coburn, they were carrying milk to Boston when captured by advance British scouts near the Menotomy River at the Cambridge-Arlington dividing line. It should be noted that Smith had sent out a small party of scouts in advance of his marching column. These scouts included Lieutenant William Sutherland of the 38th Regiment, Lieutenant Adair of the marines, and Surgeon's Mate Sims of the 43rd Regiment. They were later joined by Lieutenant Grant of the artillery. The names of the enlisted advance men are uncertain but they may have been all volunteers, as was Lt. Sutherland.

At first Lt. Sutherland appears to have been on foot as was Lt. Adair. Later Sutherland mounted a horse, either his, which he had been leading, or one he had confiscated from the several countrymen the advance group had captured. Lt. Adair later got into a chaise.

In the meantime, the main body moved steadily along the road in column formation. They marched as silently as possible along a route which would lead from the water's edge in East Cambridge through the western end of Charlestown, now Somerville, and onto a road skirting the northern part of Cambridge into Menotomy, now called Arlington. Later they would march through Lexington and the outskirts of Lincoln before entering Concord.

Aside from the barking of dogs, everything seemed at first to be in order. The houses were mainly darkened with only an occasional light here and there. There is no way, however, that 700 or so soldiers, accompanied by a number of horses, can move in complete silence. More than one colonial was awakened by the sound of the soldiers' measured tread. Many a concerned New England face peered out from behind the window frames of numerous farmhouses on that frosty moonlit night in April. Motivated by the common cause, more than one Yankee man hastily donned his clothing, saddled his horse, and sped to the house of his militia or minute company captain. In this setting, the words "Captain, the Regulars are out" must have transformed many a rustic leader into action.

As the British passed through the moon-bathed night, they sent out patrols to investigate the occasional light they saw. They also sent a patrol to investigate the Black Horse Tavern in Menotomy. At this tavern, three Marblehead men, Colonel Jeremiah Lee, Colonel Azor Orne and Elbridge Gerry, all members of the Committee of Safety, were spending the night. As the British approached the front door, the New England gentlemen fled out the back door where they lay prone in the stubble of a cornfield until the danger had passed.

In the center of Menotomy, Smith halted his main column. It was here that he most likely sent ahead the six companies of light infantry under Major John Pitcairn. It was their job to secure the North and South Bridges in Concord. He also sent back to General Gage in Boston a request for reinforcements.[17] It seems that he had heard, or was told of, the alarm guns which the Provincial militia had fired. In a letter dated April 27, 1775, to General Gage's secretary, Lt. William Sutherland mentioned that he had heard several shots between 3:00 and 4:00 in the morning, "a very unusual time for firing."[18] Sutherland heard these shots while he was with the advance scouts, and information relating to these shots would have been sent back to Smith. Therefore, Smith must have known that he had lost all hope of surprising the guardians of the military stores in Concord.

There were many alarm riders responsible for the loss of Smith's element of surprise. Doubtless the most famous was Paul Revere, who was immortalized in the poem "Paul Revere's Ride" by the 19th century New England poet, Henry Wadsworth Longfellow. Ironically, Revere himself failed to reach the town of Concord with news that the British were heading that way, as he was captured by an advance British patrol in Lincoln before he even reached the Concord line. Thanks to Longfellow's poem, Paul Revere is, perhaps, the most well-known personage

---

[17] Coburn, p. 54.

[18] Allen French, General Gage's Informers, The University of Michigan Press, Ann Arbor, 1932, pp. 43-44.

associated with the events of April 19, 1775. Therefore, his famous ride deserves some attention to detail.

In April of 1775, the forty-year-old Revere was known to the British. He had served as a dispatch rider for the Selectmen of Boston following the Boston Tea Party on December 16, 1773. As noted earlier, Revere along with about 30 mechanics had served on a committee of observation, whose purpose was the gaining of intelligence concerning future British plans in and around Boston. On April 16, Revere had noticed the British preparations for the Concord operation. As a trusted Patriot and experienced express rider, Revere was one of two men chosen by Dr. Joseph Warren to ride into the country to alert the rural residents of the British expedition.

In addition to his concern for the Concord military stores, Dr. Warren feared for the safety of the two Patriot leaders, Samuel Adams and John Hancock. Adams and Hancock on the evenings of April 18 were staying in Lexington at the home of the Reverend Jonas Clarke. As this residence was not far from the road the British would take on their way to Concord, Dr. Warren thought it likely that the British might send a patrol over to the Rev. Clarke's house to capture the two men, both members of the Second Provincial Congress, which had adjourned in Concord on April 15. It should be noted that many people at the time thought that the British expedition Smith led had a dual purpose, which was the destruction of the Provincial military stores and the arrest of Samuel Adams and John Hancock. The documentary evidence that this writer has seen, however, is too flimsy to emphatically state that the British mission included the arrest of Adams and Hancock. Gage's written orders to Smith concerned only the destruction of the Provincial military stores and the safeguarding of private property. There was no mention of Adams and Hancock or their arrest. What oral instructions Gage gave to Smith is, of course, another matter entirely.

In any event, Revere left Dr. Warren and prepared for his vital mission. He knew he would not be the only alarm rider to leave Boston for Dr. Warren had dispatched William Dawes earlier. The thirty-year-old Dawes, also an experienced express rider in the common cause, took the longer land route out of Boston, which took him over Roxbury neck and through the towns of Brookline and Cambridge until he reached the road to Concord in Menotomy.

Paul Revere, who among his trades included that of silversmith, was a mixture of strong French Huguenot and Yankee stock. He knew that the British would try to stop him and that Dr. Warren had chosen him as insurance in the event Dawes was captured. Upon leaving Dr. Warren, Revere arranged that two lanterns be displayed by a friend as a prearranged signal to Colonel Conant and other Whigs on the Charlestown shore that the British were leaving Boston by the water route. Had the British taken the land route, as William Dawes had, Revere's friend would have displayed one lantern. According to tradition, the signal lanterns were displayed from the steeple of the Christ Church, which is also known as the North Church. In the event Revere and Dawes were captured before they left Boston, the watching patriots on the Charlestown shore would see the signal and send their own messengers to spread the alarm.

By prearrangement, Revere met with two men, Joshua Bentley and Thomas Richardson, who were to row him across the Charles to the Charlestown shore. According to Revere family tradition, the three patriots had forgotten to bring material to muffle the oars. One of Revere's companions had a girlfriend who lived along the way to Revere's concealed boat. From this fair "Daughter of Liberty" the men obtained a petticoat still warm from the wearer's body, or so the tradition goes.

With muffled oars, Revere was rowed across the Charles on a flood tide under a rising moon. The three men crossed the Charles seaward of the Somerset, a large British frigate of 64 guns. Despite the rising moon, the patriots were not hailed by the watch on the frigate, who may have been looking upriver where the army was crossing. In any event, Revere was safely landed near Charlestown Battery, where he soon made contact with other patriots.

Revere was soon loaned a good horse by John Larkin, a wealthy Charlestown citizen.[19] He was also warned by Richard Devens, Esq. to be on the alert for an armed mounted patrol of nine British officers. Devens had seen the British patrol earlier in the evening after sunset heading toward Concord.[20]

Paul Revere's account of his ride from Charlestown to Lexington follows in his own words:

"I set off, it was then about 11 o'clock, the moon shone bright. I had got almost over Charlestown Common, towards Cambridge, when I saw two officers on horseback, standing under the shade of a tree, in a narrow part of the road. I was near enough to see their holsters and cockades. One of them started his horse towards me, the other up the road, as I supposed, to head me should I escape the first. I turned my horse short about, and rid upon a full gallop for Mistick Road, he followed me about 300 yards, and finding he could not catch me, returned. I proceeded to Lexington, through Mistick, and alarmed Mr. Adams and Col. Hancock."[21]

It should be noted that this sudden encounter with the two British mounted officers forced Revere to detour from his original course on the shortest route to Menotomy; at the top of Winter Hill he bore right into Medford, making his trip to Lexington a few miles longer. As he rode through Medford he alerted almost every household along the way including that of the Captain of the Medford Minute Men, Isaac Hall. The road took Revere to the center of Menotomy where at Cooper's Tavern he turned northwesterly towards Lexington.[22] When he arrived at the Rev. Jonas Clarke's house in Lexington, Revere was greeted by orderly Sergeant William Munroe of the

---

[19] Esther Forbes, Paul Revere and the World He Lived In, Houghton Mifflin Co., Boston, 1942, p. 257.

[20] Sawtell, "Paul Revere's Account," p. 221.

[21] Sawtell, "Paul Revere's Account," pp. 221-222.

[22] Coburn, pp. 24-25.

Lexington Militia Company and an eight-man guard. Earlier on the evening of Tuesday, April 18, Munroe had been told by Solomon Brown that he had seen nine armed British officers on the road heading toward Lexington from Boston. Thinking that the purpose of the British patrol was the capture of Hancock and Adams, Munroe gathered a guard together and posted his men at the Rev. Clarke's home.[23]

According to William Munroe's written deposition of March 7, 1825, Paul Revere rode up to Rev. Clarke's home about midnight and requested admittance. Munroe replied that

"the family had just retired, and had requested that they might not be disturbed by any more noise about the house. Munroe remembered Revere's reply as follows: 'Noise! You'll have noise enough before long. The Regulars are coming out.'"[24]

Having alerted Hancock and Adams of the British approach, Revere waited for William Dawes who rode up about a half hour after Revere's arrival at Rev. Clarke's Lexington parsonage. The two express riders started towards Concord and were soon overtaken by Dr. Samuel Prescott. According to the accepted tradition, young Dr. Prescott of Concord had been visiting his sweetheart Miss Mulliken of Lexington. As he was familiar with the road and many of the residents along it, Dr. Prescott was accepted by Revere and Dawes as a valuable addition to their company. Revere informed the two other riders of what Mr. Devens had told him earlier in Charlestown of the nine-man British patrol he saw heading towards Concord. As Revere had not as yet met up with the patrol, he was alert to the good possibility that the patrol was still between the three riders and Concord.

---

[23] Elias Phinney, History of the Battle at Lexington on the Morning of the 19th April 1775, "William Munroe's Affidavit of March 7, 1825," Phelps and Farnham, Boston, 1825, p. 33.

[24] Ibid.

Indeed the British mounted patrol was in waiting along the road in Lincoln, west of Josiah Nelson's farmhouse. This was the same patrol that Solomon Brown had seen earlier in the afternoon headed towards Concord. Under the command of Major Edward Mitchell of the 5th Regiment, the mission of this patrol was to stop and detain anyone they met along the road who might warn the guardians of the military stores in Concord. In fact, Major Mitchell's patrol had already detained a smaller patrol sent out earlier in the evening by Sergeant William Munroe of Lexington. The Lexington patrol, consisting of Jonathan Loring, Elijah Sanderson, and the before-mentioned Solomon Brown, had hoped to gain intelligence as to the larger British patrol's purpose. Instead, the three Lexington militia men were themselves captured by Mitchell's patrol in Lincoln on the road "just before Brooks."[25] According to Elijah Sanderson's December 17, 1824, affidavit, the three men started on their patrol about 9 o'clock. An earlier deposition signed by three men on April 25, 1775, indicated the time of their capture as about 10 o'clock.[26] In addition, Mitchell's patrol had detained a pedlar who had been out on the road.

Suspecting, but not knowing the location of the British road trap ahead of them, Revere and his two companion riders continued in the direction of Concord alerting the residents along the road. At about the Lexington-Lincoln line, Prescott and Dawes had stopped at a house to "awake the man."[27] This home was probably not far east of Josiah Nelson's Lincoln farmhouse. By his own account, Revere was about 200 yards ahead of Prescott and Dawes when they stopped. Suddenly Revere saw two British officers under a tree. In his own words Revere described what followed in the final draft of his deposition:

---

[25] Ibid., "Affidavit of Elijah Sanderson, Dec. 17, 1824," Appendix No. 1, p. 31.

[26] Vincent J. R. Kehoe, We Were There! The American Rebels, "Deposition of Jonathan Loring, Solomon Brown, and Elijah Sanderson, April 25, 1775," p. 80.

[27] Sawtell, "Paul Revere's Account," p. 222.

"I called to my company to come up, saying here was two of them, in an instant, I saw four of them, who rode up to me with their pistols in their hands and said G-d d-n you stop, if you go an inch further, you are a dead man. Immediately Mr. Prescott came up we attempted to git thro them, but they kept before us, and swore if we did not turn in to that pasture, they would blow our brains out (at this point in his first draft Revere had written "they had placed themselves opposite to a pair of Barrs, and had taken the Barrs down"), they forced us in, when we had got in, Mr. Prescot said put on. He took to the left, I to the right towards a Wood, at the bottom of the Pasture intending, when I gained that, to jump my Horse and run affoot; just as I reached it, out started six officers, siesed my bridle, put their pistols to my Breast, ordered me to dismount, which I did."[28]

And so, unlike Henry Wadsworth Longfellow's fictional account of "Paul Revere's Ride" which ended in Concord, the actual ride ended in a Lincoln pasture some four miles or so short of the center of Concord. But what of Dr. Prescott and William Dawes?

Revere does not say what happened to Dawes, but the first draft of his deposition mentioned that Dr. Prescott "turned to the left-jumped his horse over the wall and got to Concord."[29] Students of the action on April 18 and 19th are well aware of the Hartwell Family traditional story of how Dr. Prescott escaped from the British and made his way to the back door of the Samuel Hartwell farmhouse about a half mile eastward in Lincoln. We will get back to Dr. Prescott and the remainder of his ride later, but first let's see what happened to William Dawes.

Apparently, Dawes never wrote an account of his arduous ride. Some years later, however, his daughter wrote an account of her father's adventurous evening, which appeared in 1878 and was reprinted, in part, in Leland J. Abel and Cordelia Thomas Snow's 1966 archeological report of two sites that were

---

[28] Ibid., pp. 222-223.

[29] Ibid., p. 223.

excavated in the vicinity of Revere's capture site. Dawes' daughter wrote in part:

> *"He then set out to Concord with his friend, but they shortly met a party of English soldiers and officers who attempted their capture; and it was on this occasion, I think, becoming separated from Mr. Revere, and hotly pursued by three or four men, my father galloped furiously to a farmhouse a little way from the road, and, as though confident of aid, called aloud to the inmates to assist him to capture the red-coats, who alarmed at once drew back, and my father, who had been thrown to the ground by the suddenness with which he had been forced to check his horse, found on rising that he was quite empty."*[30]

According to the Dawes's tradition, Dawes lost his pocket watch when he was unseated from his horse, but the watch was later recovered.

The location of the empty house whose yard Dawes entered was uncertain for many years. The last occupied house Revere, Dawes, and Prescott passed, however, was probably that of Josiah Nelson in Lincoln on what is now (1983) Nelson Road located within Minute Man National Historical Park. The Josiah Nelson house was destroyed by fire in 1908 leaving the remains of the chimney. In 1964 two shallow depressions were found about 100 yards west of the Josiah Nelson house site. One of these depressions was close to the road. Further research and archeological investigation revealed that the southern of the two depressions might have been the abandoned house William Dawes rode up to in the early morning hours of April 19, 1775. This house had been owned by Daniel Brown, who vacated the property before 1762. In 1770 Brown sold it to Josiah Nelson, who lived until his death in 1810 in the house about 100 yards east of the one he bought from Brown.[31] It is possible that

---

[30] Leland J. Abel and Cordelia Thomas Snow, The Excavation of Sites 22 and 23, Minute Man National Historical Park, Massachusetts, National Park Service, 1966, p. 5.

[31] Ibid., p. 3.

Nelson failed to find a tenant for the former Brown home and used it for storage in 1775. This is, of course, conjecture.

If the abandoned house Dawes rode up to was indeed the house vacated by Daniel Brown, it was probably not too far eastward of the actual site of Revere's capture. Revere, of course, stated in his account that he was 200 yards ahead of Dawes and Prescott, who had stopped at a house "to awake the man."[32] According to a Lincoln tradition, Dawes and Prescott stopped at a house near the Lexington/Lincoln line where they found Nathaniel Baker, a Lincoln Minute Man, courting Elizabeth Taylor, who was a guest in the house. As Josiah Nelson's was the last occupied house in this vicinity, the house Dawes and Prescott stopped at could not have been too far eastward of the house Josiah Nelson occupied.

On the other hand, the statement Elijah Sanderson made at the age of seventy-three, some 49 years later, seems to support the theory that the Revere capture site is considerably westward of the present monument. According to Sanderson, the British had set up their road trap "just before we got to Brooks in Lincoln,"[33] and that the British detained the three Lexington men "in that vicinity" until 2:15 a.m. on that moonlit Wednesday morning in April. The phrase "in the vicinity" may refer to the woods adjoining the field where Revere was later captured when he rode up with Dawes and Prescott following about 200 yards behind. Sanderson's statement mentions that while he and his two companions were under detention, the British patrol captured Revere and Allen, a one-handed pedlar. According to Sanderson, the British interrogated Revere within a half rod of where Sanderson and his captives were held captive.

In 1775, the nearest Brooks home was located perhaps 1.5 miles westward along the road from the monument, which presently (1983) marks the site of Paul Revere's capture. This monument is located along a relatively straight stretch of the

---

[32] Sawtell, "Paul Revere's Account," p. 222.

[33] Phinney, "Affidavit Elijah Sanderson, Dec. 17, 1824," Appendix No. 1, p 31.

road with fairly level land to the south of the road opposite the monument. To the north of the road at this point, the land is fairly level for about 100 paces and then it drops off in a steep incline. Although the area of the monument on both sides of the road has been disturbed somewhat by the 20th century works of man, extant late 19th century photographs show it to be fairly level. In his 1798 letter to Jeremy Belknap, Revere mentions that the British road trap was placed in a straight road which inclined each way.

If the dual purpose of Smith's expedition was to capture Hancock and Adams, why didn't Mitchell place his road trap east of Lexington Common to prevent anyone from alarming the two Patriot leaders of the British approach? Instead, he chose a poor location west of Lexington, as evidenced by the escape of Dawes and Prescott. To be effective, a good road trap is usually set up around a bend in the road with natural barriers on either side to prevent the intended victim's escape

Revere, in any event, was captured in Lincoln short of the Concord line, Dawes escaped and by tradition went back to Lexington, while Dr. Prescott evaded the British patrol by turning his horse to the left and jumping a wall.

Concord's Dr. Prescott must have known this section of Lincoln fairly well. According to tradition, he evaded the British horsemen in a swamp, and circled northward through a thicket and then westward where he next reappeared at the back door of Samuel Hartwell's house about a half mile or so westward along the road in Lincoln. Hartwell, a sergeant in Captain William Smith's Lincoln minute man company, Mary, the twenty-seven-year-old wife of Samuel Hartwell, and Sukey, the slave-girl were all awakened.[34] (It should be noted that recent historians can find no trace of Sukey, the slave-girl in any of the Lincoln town records they have examined). Prescott informed the Hartwells of his brush with the patrol and the approach of the British from Boston. According to the Hartwell family tradition, as related by Hersey, Mary Hartwell told Sukey to run to Captain William

---

[34] Frank W. C. Hersey, Heroes of the Battle Road, Perry Walton, Boston, 1930, p. 21.

Smith's house, her neighbor to the east, and warn Captain Smith of the British approach. Sukey, according to the tradition, refused to go out of fear of the British. It is said that Mary handed her baby to Sukey and throwing on a cloak, went out into the night to warn the neighboring minute man captain of the pending danger. In the meantime, Samuel Hartwell dressed and saw that his military equipment was in readiness.[35]

It should be noted that the above traditional account is based upon conversations author Frank Hersey had with Jonas and Samuel Hartwell, both grandsons of Mary Hartwell. It seems that Mary had entertained her grandchildren by telling them stories related to her experiences on April 19, 1775. Hersey, of course, was hearing these stories second-hand many years after the fact. Therefore, they should be viewed in the realm of family tradition and not well-documented history.

The careful student of the Hartwell family tradition should note that there is another version of the above story by another 19th century writer, Abram English Brown. In his 1896 publication, Beneath Old Roof Trees, Brown's account of the story Mary Hartwell told her grandchildren differs in detail from the story related by Hersey. According to Brown's account, Mary Hartwell first learned of the British approach from a colored lady who lived next door. According to Brown's version, the black lady was afraid to go any further, so Mary left her baby with her and spread the warning herself. According to Mary's account in this version she spotted the British troops coming up the road in "fine order."[36]

Abram E. Brown obtained his information from the grandsons of Mary Hartwell as did Frank Hersey. Brown published his account in 1896 while Hersey did not publish his until 1930. Hersey must have known his version was different from Brown's earlier account, but nevertheless he published it.

---

[35] Ibid., pp. 21-22.

[36] Abram English Brown, Beneath Old Roof Trees, Lee and Shepard Publishers, Boston, 1896, p. 320.

Perhaps he had good reasons, but historians have failed to find documentation supporting the existence of the slave-girl Sukey. There is, however, documentation in Ephraim Hartwell's 1786 will to support the existence of his slave Violet.[37]

The inference, of course, is that if the Samuel Hartwell family was first alerted by Violet, and not Dr. Prescott, the good doctor must have bypassed Sam Hartwell's back door and alerted the people at Ephraim Hartwell's Tavern. If this is true, Professor Hersey's version in Heroes of the Battle Road is wrong.

In this writer's view, it would have been more natural for Dr. Prescott to have gone to a public tavern, especially one whose owner was a former influential member of the militia, than to a private residence. However, the time frame for the British Army marching up the road in Brown's version is all wrong. The British could not have passed the Hartwell residences in Lincoln until 6 a.m., while Dr. Prescott must have arrived in the Hartwell neighborhood before 2 o'clock.

In the house immediately to the west of Sam Hartwell's house, Sam's father Ephraim maintained a country tavern. Ephraim, a former Cornet in the militia, at age sixty-eight was too old for military service in 1775. His son John, however, who also resided in the house along with Elizabeth, Ephraim's wife, and Violet, a slave woman, was a sergeant also in Captain Smith's Lincoln Minute Man Company. John Hartwell, like his brother Sam, would be marching in the ranks of their Lincoln Minute Man Company before the night was over.

In any event, shortly after he was awakened by Mrs. Mary Hartwell, Captain William Smith, the twenty-nine-year-old brother of Abigail Adams, mounted his horse and rode quickly to Lincoln Center, some two miles to the south, where he would assemble his minute man company. According to tradition, Nathaniel Baker had awakened a number of Lincoln Minute Men

---

[37] John Luzader, Samuel Hartwell House and Ephraim Hartwell Tavern, National Park Service, 1968, p. 21.

who resided in houses along the route to the Baker Farm in South Lincoln.[38]

Dr. Prescott had, of course, departed the Hartwell's neighborhood and set off for Concord. Historian Allen French discounts the traditional story, recorded earlier by Lemuel Shattuck, an earlier Concord historian, that Dr. Prescott first rode to the center of Lincoln, before proceeding on to Concord.[39] It is obvious that a ride to Lincoln Center was not only miles out of Prescott's way, but it would have been entirely unnecessary, as he had discharged his obligation to Lincoln by alerting Baker and Sergeant Samuel Hartwell. In any event, according to the diary statement of the Concord minister, William Emerson, Concord received the alarm between one and two o'clock on the evening of April 19, 1775.[40] (French, a close student of the events that occurred in Concord on April 19, discounted the written statement Amos Barrett made some 50 years later that the alarm was sounded at three o'clock.) As the Concord tradition goes, Amos Melven, a member of the guard Colonel Barrett had placed near the center of Concord, saw to it, or rang the bell in alarm himself. Concord would soon know that the British were coming and her men quickly dressed and took up their arms.

Earlier, as I have indicated, Paul Revere had been captured by the advance British patrol in Lincoln. He was detained in a field somewhere west of Josiah Nelson's residence and east of Samuel Hartwell's farm. The British kept Revere separated from the three-man Lexington patrol and one-handed pedlar they had captured before Revere rode into their trap. The latter four men had been detained in the woods adjoining the field where Revere had been halted. The British questioned Revere closely during

[38] Hersey, p. 12.

[39] Allen French, The Day of Concord and Lexington, Little Brown, Boston, 1925, pp. 148-149.

[40] William Emerson, Diary "Proceedings at the Centennial Celebration of Concord's Fight," Concord, 1876, facing p. 164.

the period of his detention. At one point of his interrogation, a British officer, who Revere later learned was Major Edward Mitchell, put his pistol to Revere's head and threatened to blow the patriot's brains out unless he got the truth to his questions.[41]

After the British had interrogated Revere, they ordered him and their other four prisoners to mount up. According to Elijah Sanderson, the British and their prisoners started their ride eastward to Lexington about quarter past two in the morning of a pleasant moonlit night. Sanderson's 1824 affidavit states that the British were riding at considerable speed and one of the officers struck Sanderson's horse with his hanger to make the horse go faster. The British rode on each side of their prisoners.[42] According to Revere's account, he was not trusted with reins and was led by an officer who moved to the front of the patrol.

As the British and their five prisoners returned to Lexington, they had to re-pass the home of Josiah Nelson. An interesting Nelson family tradition has developed concerning the interaction of Josiah Nelson and Major Mitchell's patrol. According to this tradition, as retold by Frank W. C. Hersey in his 1930 publication, Heroes of the Battle Road, Josiah Nelson was awakened by his wife, who apparently mistook the returning British patrol for farmers going along the Old Bay Road (this writer has also seen the road referred to as the Country Road, County Road, or road to Boston, Lexington, Concord, etc., depending on one's view of it) to market their milk or whatever. (It has always interested this writer how Nelson could have slept through the earlier shouts of Revere, Dawes and Prescott, especially if Dawes had earlier shouted for help at the abandoned house only 100 yards west of Josiah Nelson's occupied house.) However, to return to our traditional story, Nelson is said to have slipped into his breeches and, hatless and shoeless, rushed

---

[41] Sawtell, "Paul Revere's Account," pp. 224-225.

[42] Phinney, "Affidavit of Elijah Sanderson, Dec. 17, 1824," p. 32.

out among the moving horseman shouting "Have you heard anything about when the Regulars are coming out?"[43] (Both the accounts of Revere and Sanderson state that the British patrol started back at a good rate of speed. They must have slowed down or Nelson would not have rashly rushed out among galloping horses.) In any event, one of the British officers, by tradition Major Mitchell, drew his saber and yelled "We will let you know when they are coming."[44] With those words the officer is said to have inflicted a gash on the crown of Nelson's head with a glancing blow from his saber. If this traditional story is true, the first blood to be drawn by an opponent on the first day of the Revolutionary War belonged to that of Josiah Nelson of the Lincoln Minute Men.

After receiving his wound from the hot-tempered British officer, the bleeding Nelson was ordered to walk between the British horsemen, who were now content it seems to progress towards Lexington at a slower pace. According to the Nelson family tradition, there were also three Tories in Major Mitchell's patrol, who had been acting as guides. As the lame Nelson on foot could not keep up with the patrol, Major Mitchell left him in the charge of the three Tories. The Tories were known to Nelson, although the Nelson family tradition does not name them. In any case, they decided to let their countryman go with the warning, "Go back to your house and stay there and don't light a light. If you give any alarm or light a light, we will burn your house over your head."[45]

The story goes that Nelson returned to his house where he lit a candle and had his wound dressed by his wife. He then, according to tradition, loaded his horse pistols and, after saddling his mare, galloped off to Bedford by the back road to spread the alarm.

---

[43] Hersey, p. 18.

[44] Hersey, p. 18.

[45] Hersey, pp. 18-19.

The Nelson family tradition has come down to us in Hersey's Heroes of the Battle Road and is apparently based on stories George Nelson, Josiah Nelson's grandson, told to Frank Hersey prior to the publication of the latter's little book in 1930. As with many family traditions, details are often distorted; however, so much of the lore surrounding April 19, 1775, is based on either tradition or biased statements from participants, the student of that fateful day in our history must consider traditional accounts for what they are worth. To leave them out would delete much of the color and human interest from a story which has fascinated historians and others who have given their attention to that day, which saw fired the first shots of the Revolutionary War. It is interesting to note, however, that neither Paul Revere's three accounts, nor Elijah Sanderson's lengthy 1824 account, or the shorter accounts signed on April 25, 1775 by Solomon Brown, Jonathan Loring, or Elijah Sanderson mention Josiah Nelson or anyone fitting his description as having received a saber cut from a British officer on the ride back to Lexington on the early evening hours of April 19, 1775. Had this incident occurred, why did not Revere or one of the other American prisoners of the British patrol mention it in their accounts?

As every student of April 19, 1775, should know, the Provincial leaders in the days immediately following the outbreak of fighting, obtained written depositions from American participants and witnesses to the effect that the British were the aggressors who fired first at Lexington and Concord. How then did the American deposition gatherers miss the incident involving Josiah Nelson and the saber swinging British officer? It would seem that this unprovoked and brutal attack by a hot-tempered British officer on a Massachusetts citizen was not included in the formal American depositions of the time. Perhaps, it had been overlooked by the committee set up to gather depositions, whose main purpose appeared to be to absolve the Massachusetts militia leaders for any blame for the fighting on Lexington Common and Concord's North Bridge.

Let's return now to the British patrol which had again picked up its pace since the lame Nelson had been released. According to Revere, the officer who had been leading Revere's horse turned the reins over to a sergeant who was ordered to shoot Revere should he try to escape. As the patrol approached within about a half mile of the Lexington meeting house, a shot was heard. Major Mitchell asked Revere about the meaning of the shot and Revere replied that it was to alarm the county. Mitchell then halted the patrol and ordered the pedlar and three men from Lexington to dismount. One of his officers also dismounted and cut the bridles and saddles off the four prisoners' horses before driving them away. Revere asked Mitchell for his release, but the major refused, and ordered the patrol in motion once again.[46]

As the British patrol got within sight of the meeting house, a musket volley was heard. Once more Major Mitchell ordered the patrol to halt. The worried British officer then asked Revere how far it was to Cambridge. Mitchell then asked the sergeant if his horse was tired and, when the sergeant replied yes, the Major ordered him to take Revere's horse, which must have been a good horse to stand up so well after the hard riding it had received since it left Charlestown about four hours earlier. Revere dismounted and the sergeant mounted the patriot's borrowed horse. The bridle and saddle of the horse the sergeant had been riding was cut away and the British rode off in the direction of Cambridge. Revere was now free and he proceeded in the direction of the Rev. Jonas Clarke's house to tell Samuel Adams and John Hancock what had happened to him.[47]

Major Mitchell's decision to release Paul Revere, a man known to him as an enemy of the Crown, was doubtless based on the difficult circumstances in which he found himself and his mounted patrol. From the shots that he had heard, he knew that an armed Provincial force had gathered near the meeting house in Lexington. He knew that his relatively small patrol would have to pass in the vicinity of this colonial force on its way to meet the

---

[46] Sawtell, "Paul Revere's Account," pp. 226-227.

[47] Sawtell, "Paul Revere's Account," p. 227.

advancing British column from Boston. It would surely prove awkward to him if he was taken by the numerically superior Yankees with the noted rebel, Paul Revere, under his custody. He could also increase the mobility of his patrol by releasing Revere in the event he had to make a dash for it. He must have thought also that his main duty now was to alert Lt. Col. Smith of the armed rebels waiting for him near Lexington Common and the fact that Concord was probably alarmed due to the escape of the young Yankee rider at the Lincoln road trap.

As related earlier, Paul Revere had alerted Hancock and Adams, along with their guards from the Lexington Militia about midnight. It was not long after Revere's warning that the bell in the belfry on Lexington Common rang out the alarm. Soon the members of Captain John Parker's Lexington Militia Company began to assemble on the Common. According to the muster role compiled by Frank Coburn, Captain Parker's full company contained 144 men.[48] According to Lexington historian Elias Phinney, most of Parker's company had mustered by 2 a.m. While he had his men on parade, Captain Parker ordered them to charge their muskets with powder and ball. He had sent several scouts on the road to Boston and when one returned reporting that he saw no sign of the British, the forty-five-year-old Parker probably doubted if the British were indeed coming his way. Standing on parade in the chill night air, Parker realized his men were beginning to feel the cold. He, therefore, dismissed them around two o'clock or shortly thereafter. He told them to reassemble, however, at the beat of a drum. Those who lived near the Common went home, but those who lived beyond the sound of a drum retired to the shelter of the nearby Buckman Tavern. Traditionally, historians have recorded the number of men who answered the first alarm as 130. According to Elias Phinney writing in 1825, the greater part of Captain Parker's men went into the tavern.[49] Not all remained inside, however, as Paul

---

[48] Frank Warren Coburn, The Battle on Lexington Common: April 19, 1775, F. L. Coburn & Co., Boston, 1921, pp. 31-32.

[49] Phinney, p. 18.

Revere reported an alarm volley was fired when he and his captors got within sight of the meeting house.

As the reader will recall, this writer left Lt. Col. Frances Smith and his force in the center of Menotomy. Smith had detached six companies of the Light Infantry ahead of his main column to secure Concord's North and South Bridges. In advance of the six companies of Light Infantry under Major Pitcairn, the small advance scouts with Lt. Sutherland, Lt. Adair, and others progressed toward Lexington. According to tradition, three Tories served as guides for the British force and were also with the advance party. Included among these Loyalists was said to be Concord's Daniel Bliss. In the extreme forward position of the British column, in what we call the "point" today, the British sent several soldiers ahead. According to Elias Phinney, these soldiers would conceal themselves along either side of the road. When a person approached, they would let him pass and then rise, trapping the unsuspecting man between them and the advance scouts.[50] This was the method they probably used to capture Benjamin Wellington about two miles east of Lexington Common. Wellington was one of several scouts Captain John Parker had sent out along the road to Boston to report on the progress of the British advance.

As the British forward scouts moved toward their objective, they were met by the advance British patrol led by Major Mitchell. Included also in this patrol were Captain Charles Cochrane of the 4th Regiment of Foot, Captain Charles Lumm of the 38th Regiment of Foot, and other mounted British officers and Sergeants. According to Lt. Sutherland, Major Mitchell told the officers in the advance party that the whole country was alarmed and that they had to gallop for their lives. Later, according to Sutherland's account, a gentleman rode up in a sukey and reported to the British that 600 men were assembled at Lexington to oppose the British. Sutherland and the advance party waited until Major Pitcairn rode up with the six detached Light Infantry companies. The man in the sukey repeated the

[50] Ibid., pp. 18-19.

disturbing news to Major Pitcairn, after which Sutherland rode ahead again, where he soon captured another colonial night rider.[51] No wonder Captain Parker remained in doubt as to the British approach.

Following his capture of the lone rider, Sutherland met some men with a wagon containing wood. From these men, the Lieutenant was told that 1,000 armed men awaited the British in Lexington. Later the British officer saw what he described as a "vast number" of armed militia going over a hill toward Lexington. The energetic Sutherland with assistance from Lt. Adair captured one of the militiamen and confiscated his firelock and bayonet.[52]

After disarming the colonial militiaman, Sutherland and the advance party turned back where they found Pitcairn's Light Infantry force halted on the road. Apparently, the major was concerned by the news he had received from the man in the sukey and was organizing his troops into a better disposition to deal with the expected threat ahead of him in Lexington. The Marine Major alertly put out flankers and advance men to better protect his six Light Infantry companies. We know that Pitcairn on the way out had depended on Sutherland, Adair, and a mixed collection of Tories, officers from various regiments, and enlisted men as advance scouts. In the final stages of the approach to Lexington, Sutherland informs us that the front party consisted of a Sergeant and six or eight men. He and Lt. Adair rode on with this advance guard, which Pitcairn had apparently reorganized during the period he halted the six Light Infantry companies.[53]

As Sutherland proceeded along with the advance guard, he heard the report of shots to his right and left. As he did not hear

---

[51] Harold Murdock, Ed., <u>Late News of the Excursion and Ravages of the King's Troops on the Nineteenth of April 1775</u>, "Lt. William Sutherland's Narratives, April 26, 1775," Harvard Press, Cambridge, 1927, p. 15.

[52] Ibid., pp. 15-16.

[53] Ibid., p. 16.

the "whissing" of balls he concluded that they were alarm shots. At one point when the British were in Sutherland's words "within gunshot of Lexington," he says that a man on the right side of the road aimed his piece at him, but the gun misfired and only burnt the priming charge in the pan.[54] Major Pitcairn was soon informed of this incident and it must have been on his mind when he heard the roll of the drum from Lexington Common calling the militia to parade. It was at this point that he probably ordered his men to charge their weapons with powder and ball.

According to Orderly Sergeant William Munroe's 1825 affidavit, the British "charged their pieces" when they heard the roll of the alarm drum. Munroe pinpointed this position with some accuracy as later in the day he walked the area and saw the ends of some two hundred paper cartridges the British had spit on the ground after they had ripped them open with their teeth.[55] Two hundred cartridge ends would be fairly consistent with the number of men in Pitcairn's advance company of Light Infantry. Ensign Jeremy Lester of His Majesty's 10th Regiment of Foot stated in his narrative that the British loaded about a half hour before they unloaded again (fired).[56] It would seem that Ensign Lester overestimated the time between loading and firing, as it should not have taken the British a half hour to advance only 100 rods (550 yards), unless there was a delay between loading and resuming the march. Munroe's statement is also supported by that of others including Captain William Soutar of the British Marines, who said the British had loaded only an instant before the firing began.[57]

---

[54] Ibid.

[55] Phinney, "William Munroe March 7, 1825 Affidavit," p. 34.

[56] Ensign Jeremy Lister, Concord Fight, Narrative of Ensign Jeremy Lister, Harvard University Press, Cambridge, 1931, p. 23.

[57] Kehoe, We Were There! The British Soldiers, "Captain William Soutar Correspondence," p. 162.

But to get back to Captain Parker and his Lexington militia. As the reader will recall, Parker had dismissed his men at some time after 2 a.m. with orders to reassemble on Lexington Common at the sound of a drum. Some went home, and perhaps even more went into the Buckman Tavern to wait where it was warmer. History is silent concerning much of what went on in and near the tavern during the few hours between the first and second alarms. Parker, however, must have been concerned that his scouts had not returned from their scouting missions along the road to Boston. Ignorance of an enemy's position and intent is always frustrating to a military commander. What plans Parker made for the defense of the town or road to Concord or what conversations he had with town officials is unclear. In any case, the last scout Captain Parker sent out, Thaddeus Bowman, soon rode up in the early morning light. Bowman had narrowly missed capture by two British soldiers concealed along the side of the road in advance of the British column. By wheeling his horse, Bowman evaded the trap and soon sped back to his captain with the news that he had sighted the British. It must have been around 5 a.m., when Captain Parker ordered William Diamond to beat the drum, which sounded the second Lexington alarm. As he watched his men reassemble on the Common, he could little realize that he and his company would soon be assured of a lasting place in their nation's history.

2 – LEXINGTON AT DAWN

As the reader of Chapter 1 will recall, we left Lt. William Sutherland just after he saw a "flash in the pan" from a musket he believed a militiaman pointed at him. It was not long after this incident that Pitcairn heard the beating of William Diamond's alarm drum and ordered the British Light Infantry companies to load their muskets. According to William Munroe's 1825 affidavit, the British charged their pieces about 100 rods east of the Meeting House.

In the meantime, Captain John Parker had ordered Orderly Sergeant William Munroe to parade the company, whose men were responding to the alarm drum. As the Lexington militiamen came onto the Common, Sergeant Munroe formed them into two ranks on the north side of the Common, or Green as we now call it.[1] The Lexington men were facing toward the road from which the British would come, but it should be noted they were not blocking the road. Captain Parker had ordered every man to load his piece with powder and ball and doubtless Sergeant Munroe insured that each man complied as he arrived at the place of parade.

---

[1] Elias Phinney, History of the Battle at Lexington on the Morning of April 19, 1775, "William Munroe's March 7, 1825 Affidavit," Phelps and Farnham, Boston, 1825, p. 34.

It should be noted that some historians record only 77 men at the second muster, while they record about 130 at the first muster earlier. What happened to the other 53 men between the two musters? Some, of course, went home and probably could not respond to the second alarm in time. According to the Lexington historian Elias Phinney, however, most of the 130 men at the first muster went to the nearby Buckman Tavern. Certainly, if they stayed in the tavern, they should have been able to make it to the second muster on time.

In any event, Captain Parker was left to face the British with only half his company, which at full strength, according to Frank Coburn, consisted of 144 men. Parker, of course, was outnumbered as the six advance Light Infantry Companies probably contained 200 men or more including the scouts and others who accompanied them. Lt. Col. Francis Smith, of course, followed behind Major Pitcairn's Light Infantry with another 500 or so men in the main body. Due to the several halts Pitcairn had made along the road since Menotomy, the gap between Pitcairn's advance force and the main body had closed considerably.

As Captain Parker watched his men fall into the two ranks, William Diamond continued his drum roll. Sergeant Munroe had formed them about six to ten rods north of the Meeting House. Some of the men had gone into the Meeting House for the purpose of replenishing their stock of powder from the town's powder, which was kept there. Perhaps this explains in part why Parker's Company was under-manned at the second muster. As Diamond's drum continued to Beat, the van of the British 10th Regiment of Foot came into view about 12 to 15 rods south of the Lexington Militia's position.[2] At this point, according to the sworn testimony given six days later by 14 participants, some of the Lexington Company were still going toward the Lexington

---

[2] Ibid., "Corporal John Munroe's Affidavit of Dec. 28, 1824," p. 35.

lines with their backs toward the British.[3] These men were probably leaving the Meeting House after replenishing their individual powder supplies.

According to Lt. Sutherland's letter of April 27, 1775, to General Thomas Gage, three shots were fired at the British "from a corner of a large house to the right of the church..."[4] The building Sutherland described as a church would, of course, have been the Meeting House. The building from whose corner the shots were fired was probably the Buckman Tavern, which would have been on Lt. Sutherland's right as he approached the Common. It should be noted that numerous American participants and witnesses testified in sworn written statements that the British fired the first shots on Lexington Common. Note, however, that the shots Sutherland records, if they occurred, did not come from the men under Captain Parker's direct control in the muster formation.

Since they had loaded their muskets east of the Meeting House, Pitcairn's Light Infantry proceeded toward the Common at a "quickstep." Some American accounts indicated that they "rushed" forward or "ran" as they poured onto the common. In any event, their appearance was too sudden for Captain Parker to form his complete company. Many of his men were still heading toward the Common when the first ranks of Pitcairn's Light Infantry moved rapidly into position before the Lexington Militia's lines. Accounts differ as to what happened next. Captain Parker's April 25, 1775, deposition in part stated:

"I ordered our militia to meet on the common in said Lexington, to consult what to do, and concluded not to be discovered, nor meddle, or make with said regular troops, if they should approach, unless they should insult or molest us; and upon their sudden approach, I immediately ordered our

---

[3] Lemuel Shattuck, A History of the Town of Concord, Russell Odiorne and Co., Boston, 1835, "Deposition of Nathaniel Parkhurst and 14 Others, April 25, 1775," pp. 344-345.

[4] Allen French, General Gage's Informers, University of Michigan Press, Ann Arbor, 1932, "Lt. Sutherland's Letter to General Gage, April 27, 1775," p. 58.

militia to disperse and not to fire. Immediately, said troops made their appearance, and rushing furiously on, fired upon and killed eight of our party, without receiving any provacation therefor from us."[5]

Note that Captain Parker said he had ordered his men to disperse before the British fired on him. This statement was supported by a deposition signed by 34 of his men only six days after the event. This deposition reads in part:

"We further testify and declare, that about five oclock in the morning, hearing our drum beat, we proceeded towards the parade, and soon found, that a large body of troops were marching towards us; some of our company began to disperse; whilst our backs were turned on the troops, we were fired on by them, and a number of our men were instantly killed and wounded. Not a gun was fired by any person in our company on the regulars to our knowledge, before they fired on us, and they continued firing until we had all made our escape."[6]

Note that the deposition states that <u>some</u> of the Lexington Militia Company began to disperse before the firing, inferring of course, that some must have stood their ground. The reader must remember that the purpose of the American depositions taken at this time was to prove that the British were the aggressors and fired first while the militia was dispersing. Some fifty years later, the citizens of Lexington resented the passive role historians in the neighboring town of Concord had assigned to the Lexington Militia. As a result, a number of depositions were taken in 1824 and 1825 in Lexington seeking to prove that the role of the Lexington Company on the morning of April 19, 1775, was not as passive as the 1775 depositions indicated. Let the reader compare the following 1825 deposition by Joseph Underwood with the preceding deposition by Captain Parker and his men.

---

[5] Shattuck, "Deposition of Captain John Parker, April 25, 1775," p. 343.

[6] Ibid., "Deposition of Nathaniel Mulliken and 33 Others, April 25, 1775," p. 344.

"When the regulars had arrived within about one hundred rods of our line, they charged their pieces and moved towards us at a quickstep. Some of our men on seeing them, proposed to quit the field, but Captain Parker gave orders for every man to stand his ground, and said he would order the first man shot, that offered to leave his post. I stood very near Captain Parker, when the regulars came up, and am confident he did not order his men to disperse, till the British troops had fired upon us the second time."[7]

The reader will recall that in Parker's deposition taken only six days after the event, the Lexington Captain stated that upon the sudden approach of the militia he immediately ordered his men to disperse. As Underwood recalls, however, Parker did not order his men to disperse until they had been fired on twice by the British.

Underwood's statement that at least a portion of the militia did not break their lines until the second British fire is supported by other depositions taken fifty years later from the Lexington veterans of the common fighting. Consider the December 28, 1824, statement of Corporal John Munroe which reads in part:

"After the first fire of the regulars, I thought, and so stated to Ebenezer Munroe, Junior, who stood next to me on the left, that they had fired nothing but powder, but on the second firing Munroe said, they had fired something more than powder, for he had received a wound in his arm; and now said he, to use his own words, 'I'll given them the guts of my gun.' We then both took arm at the main body of the British troops--the smoke preventing our seeing anything but the heads of some of their horses--and discharged our pieces."[8]

It is quite possible, of course, that Parker had, as he claimed, given the order to disperse at the sudden approach of the British. After all he would have been foolish to oppose a superior force from his exposed parade formation on the Common. Perhaps,

---

[7] Phinney, "Deposition of Joseph Underwood, dated March 7, 1825," p. 39.

[8] Phinney, "John Munroe's Affidavit of Dec. 28, 1824," pp. 36-37.

some of his men, their attention, fixed on the approaching British force, did not hear his order to disperse and stood their ground. Remember, that in an earlier order he told his men, according to several later accounts, to hold their ground. In any event, let's consider the statement of the officer who commanded the British troops on the Common, Major John Pitcairn.

In his April 26, 1775, report to his superior, General Gage, Pitcairn mentions the "flash in the pan" incident. He then states that:

"On this I gave directions to the troops to move forward, when I arrived at the end of the village, I observed drawn up upon a Green near 200 of the rebels; when I came within about one hundred yards of them, they began to file off towards some stone walls on our right flank--the Light Infantry observing this, ran after... I instantly called to the soldiers not to fire, but to surround and disarm them, and after several repetitions of those positive orders to the men, not to fire etc--some of the rebels who had jumped over the wall, fired four or five shot at the soldiers, which wounded a man of the Tenth, and my horse was wounded in two places, from some quarter or other, and at the same time several shot were fired from a Meeting House on our left...upon this, without any order or regularity, the Light Infantry began a scattered fire, and continued in that situation for some little time, contrary to the repeated orders both of me and the officers that were present."[9]

Note that Pitcairn's report seems to support Parker's deposition that the Lexington men were dispersing upon the British approach. The reader will note also that the shots did not come from the men on the Common, but from the stone wall on Pitcairn's right, from the Meeting House on his left, and from "some quarter or other." This report does not confirm a first organized British volley, but does agree with several American accounts concerning random individual fire by the British. It would also appear from Pitcairn's report that neither he or his officers had the enlisted men under control at this point.

---

[9] French, "Major Pitcairn's Letter to General Gage," p. 53.

The fact that the Americans fired on the British from behind a stone wall is confirmed by the later Lexington depositions. Nathan Munroe stated that <u>after</u> the British fired on them he "got over the wall into Buckman's land, about six rods from the British, and then turned and fired at them."[10] William Munroe also stated in a 1825 deposition that someone fired at the British from the back door of the Buckman Tavern and then, after reloading, fired at the British from the front door of the same building. Munroe states, however, that these shots were fired after the British had fired first. Sergeant Munroe also claimed that the British first fired an organized volley. He says that a British officer rode up within a few rods of his company and said "Lay down your arms you rebels and disperse." According to Munroe, the officer then fired his pistol and ordered "Fire Damn you, fire!" According to the Lexington Sergeant, the British front platoon of eight or nine men opened fire without hitting any of the Lexington company.[11]

If William Munroe's statement about the British volley not hitting anyone is correct, it is quite possible that the lead platoon fired this volley as a warning to the portion of Lexington men who had not yet dispersed. Perhaps the British troops behind the front rank, not realizing that only a warning volley had been fired, opened fire individually without orders and with deadly effect. This, of course, is conjecture, but it does explain why the first British fire apparently hurt nobody, while the random fire that followed did considerable execution.

At this point, let's return to Lt. William Sutherland's April 27, 1775, letter to General Gage and see what he says about the action on Lexington Common. As the reader will recall, Sutherland claimed a few shots were fired at the British from the corner of a large house to the right of the church (Meeting House). He goes on to say that the troops were drawn up in the plane opposite the church, when several British officers called

---

[10] Phinney, "Deposition of Nathan Munroe, dated Dec. 22, 1824," p. 38.

[11] Phinney, "William Munroe's March 7, 1825 Affidavit," p. 34.

out "throw down your arms and you shall come by no harm, or words to that effect."[12] He went on to write that officers on horseback rode in amongst the Lexington men, and he heard Major Pitcairn call out "Soldiers don't fire keep your ranks and form and surround them." He went onto add that some of the "villains" went over a hedge (stone wall) and fired at the British. In addition, Sutherland wrote that the firing set his horse into a gallop and the British officer was carried 600 yards or more down a road to his right, which took him among the middle of the militia. At last Sutherland turned his horse and he claimed that a vast number of militiamen in the woods to the right of the Grenadiers fired at him. The Lieutenant added, however, that they missed him because they were fired at a great distance. He went on to write that the Grenadiers from their position on the right flank gave the militiamen in the woods a "very smart fire."[13]

One of the militiamen who retreated up the road to the north that Sutherland's horse galloped down was Lieutenant William Tidd. According to Tidd, a mounted British officer chased him about 30 rods down the road shouting "Damn you stop, or you are a dead man!" Tidd went on to state that he jumped some bars and fired his gun at the British officer who returned to the main body of troops on the common.[14]

The accounts of Sutherland and Tidd add to the evidence that a number of militiamen took up positions to the British right behind stone walls from which they fired. Sutherland's statement is also supportive of Major Pitcairn's report to Gage in that he ordered his men not to fire on the Americans. On the conduct of the British soldiers, Lt. John Barker of the King's own Regiment provides us with a revealing look when he wrote in his diary:

---

[12] French, "Lt. Sutherland's Letter to General Gage, April 27, 1775," p. 58.

[13] Ibid., p. 141.

[14] Phinney, "Declaration of Lieutenant William Tidd, Dec. 29, 1824," p. 38.

"At 5 o'clock we arrived there (Lexington) and saw a number of people, I believe 2 to 300, formed on a common in the middle of the town; we still continued advancing, keeping prepared against an attack tho' without intending to attack them, but on our coming near them they fired one or two shots, upon which our men without any orders rushed in on them, fired and put 'em to flight; we could not tell how many because they were got behind walls and into the woods; We had a man of the 10th Light Infantry wounded, nobody else hurt."

Barker went on to add that "We then formed on the Common but with some difficulty, the men were so wild they could hear no orders."[15]

Lt. Barker's diary entry agrees with Lt. Sutherland's account that several shots were fired at the British as they approached the Common. Barker as well, confirms Pitcairn's report to General Gage that the British enlisted men fired on the Americans without orders. Barker's account also reinforces the fact, inferred in Pitcairn's report to General Gage, that the British officers had temporarily lost control of their men on Lexington Common.

The traditional view of Major John Pitcairn in American eyes was that he was a hot-tempered, saber-waving British officer with a hair-trigger temper. This view was fostered by the depositions taken within a week of the fighting under the authority of the Provincial Congress. The deposition of the Lexington Militiaman John Robbins is illustrative of this point. In part it reads:

"I being in the front rank, there suddenly appeared a number of the King's troops, about a thousand as I thought, at the distance of about sixty or seventy yards from us, huzzaing, and on a quick pace towards us, with three officers in their front on horseback, and on full gallop towards us; the foremost of which cried 'throw down your arms!--ye villains ye rebels!' upon

---

[15] Elizabeth Ellery Dana, The British in Boston, Harvard University Press, Cambridge, 1924, "Diary of Lt. John Barker, April 19, 1775," p. 32.

which, said company dispersing the foremost of the three officers ordered their men saying 'fire ___ by God ___ fire!' "[16]

In addition to giving the order to fire, several American depositions taken within a week of the fighting blame the mounted British officers for firing the first shots of the war from their pistols. The April 25, 1775, deposition of two spectators from Lexington, Levi Mead and Levi Harrington, states in part that:

"We saw a large body of regular troops marching up towards the Lexington Company, and some of the regulars on horses, whom we took to be officers, fired a pistol or two on the Lexington Company, which was then dispersing; these were the first guns that were fired, and they were immediately followed by several volleys from the regulars, by which eight men belonging to said company were killed and several wounded."[17]

As Major Pitcairn was in command of the six advanced companies of Light Infantry, it was natural for the Americans to blame him for the bloodshed on Lexington Common. It would appear, however, from the British documents, that he tried to stop his men from firing, but had simply lost control of the situation. Recent historians have been much kinder to Major Pitcairn than earlier historians, who saw him as the archetype of the cruel professional soldier. Nevertheless, he and his officers, by their own admission, lost control of their men during the initial period of firing on Lexington Common, and it took some time to calm the excited troops down.

As Lt. Sutherland's letter to Gage records, order was not restored on Lexington Common until Lt. Col. Francis Smith arrived with the main body of troops. According to Sutherland, Smith asked the Lieutenant to find a drummer, which Sutherland did. Smith then ordered the drummer to sound the appropriate

---

[16] Shattuck, "Deposition of John Robbins, April 24, 1775," p. 343.

[17] Ibid., "Deposition of Levi Mead and Levi Harrington, April 25, 1775," pp. 345-346.

roll (Beat to Arms), which eventually caused the men to reassemble into ranks. Even then somebody, according to Sutherland, fired a few shots from the gavel window from the end of the same house where Sutherland noted the first shots fired at the British.[18] Here Smith showed great restraint, as he prevented his soldiers from entering the houses near the Common, for he feared they would put all they found inside to death. In his private letter to R. Donkin written almost six months after the Lexington Common affair, Smith wrote in part:

"When the firing first began at Lexington I was going from the main body to the front of the advanced companies, was almost got there, I immediately ran up to the front, and finding the rebels scampering off, except those shut up in houses, I endeavored to the upmost to stop all further firing, which in a short time I affected, the troops then near the Meeting House and dwellings much enraged at the treatment they had received and having been fired on from the houses repeatedly, were going to break them open to come at those within, tho they deserved no favor, yet knowing if the houses were once broke into, none within could well be saved and that time thinking it possible, tho action might have been brought on by some of the rebels firing without any particular direction, I was desirous of putting a stop to all further slaughter of those deluded people, therefore gave orders, and by the assistance of some of the officers, prevented any one house being entered, and leaving them to come out with safety, marched on to Concord without firing a shot, (tho two were fired at us from the woods) and in all respects with as much good order as ever troops observed in Britain or any friendly country."[19]

From his letter, Smith appears to have acted from the highest humanitarian instincts befitting a British officer and gentleman. Upon reaching the Common, his first thoughts were to restore order and prevent further unnecessary carnage. Some historians have tried to show Smith as a corpulent incompetent of little

---

[18] French, "Lt. Sutherland's Letter to General Gage, April 27, 1775," p. 60.

[19] Vincent J. R. Kehoe, We Were There! The British Soldiers, "Letter of Lt. Col. Smith to R. Donkin, Oct. 8, 1775," p. 75.

imagination. Whatever he lacked in imagination he seemed not to lack in certain human qualities, which distinguish the true officer from the professional butcher of men.

From a close study of the available evidence, it is difficult to tell who fired the first shot at Lexington. The documentary evidence conflicts as the reader must have noted. There are other conflicts as well. For example, did the British fire an organized volley before they began their promiscuous fire? Did Captain Parker order his men to disperse before or after the British fired? Was Major Pitcairn the bloodthirsty war-monger contemporary accounts made him out to be, or did he try to prevent bloodshed as he and his officers claimed? Perhaps, the most important question is what did Captain Parker expect to accomplish with his little force from such an exposed position? This writer does not have all the answers to the above questions and others which relate to the Lexington fighting. After careful consideration, however, the following brief summary is this writer's impression of what may have occurred on Lexington Common on that fateful Wednesday morning about 5 a.m.

After loading their muskets with William Diamond's drum roll ringing in their ears, Major Pitcairn ordered his men forward at the quickstep. As they approached the Meeting House, several shots were fired by men positioned near the corner of Buckman's Tavern. These shots were either fired at the British, or perhaps even more likely, they were fired in warning to the men on the Common that the British were coming. After all, the men near the tavern would have seen the British before the men in the Lexington lines on the north side of the Common. In any event, the British 10th Regiment of Foot rushed forward onto the Common and quickly formed their disposition in front of the Lexington lines. They probably rushed to the right of the Meeting House, as this was the most direct route to the north side of the Common where the militia was formed. According to historian John R. Galvin, Pitcairn rode onto the Common from the left side of the Meeting House as he approached it, thus losing sight and control of his men.

As the front company of the Light Infantry rushed forward they shouted and huzzahed loudly. On sight of these spirited onrushing troops, Captain Parker countermanded any earlier order he may have given to stand firm and ordered his partial company to disperse. Many obeyed their Captain's command and quickly moved off the Common for the protection of a stone wall to the British right. Others, who perhaps did not hear Parker's command to disperse due to the shouting of the onrushing troops, remained in ranks facing the British. Other militiamen were in Buckman's Tavern, the Meeting House, and in the process of approaching the Common in response to the alarm drum. Just when Diamond stopped beating his drum is unclear. Perhaps, some Americans were caught in the open ground as they left the Meeting House with their powder supply on the way to the Lexington lines.

In the meantime, Major Pitcairn and several officers rode between the British and American lines. This writer believes that Pitcairn ordered the Lexington militiamen to disperse and lay down their arms. He may have even ordered the front companies not to fire, but to surround the Americans to see that they laid down their arms. What orders his officers shouted is uncertain. They may have even conflicted with the Marine Major's. In any event, some scattered shots were fired from the militiamen, who had sought protection behind the stone wall to the British right. A mounted British officer, not necessarily Pitcairn, may have fired a pistol, which was quickly followed by a British volley, probably by the men in the first rank or two of the 10th Regiment. Shots may also have come from the Meeting House on the British left. I doubt if any of Parker's men remaining in ranks on the Common fired first at the British. To do so would have been sure suicide.

Did the American shots from behind the stone wall precede the British firing on the Common? They may have, but it is not certain from the documentation that has been passed down to us. I think Lt. Sutherland made a good point in his letter to General Gage, when he said that the British soldiers would not have fired for some time for fear of hitting their own officers who galloped in among the armed militiamen. Certainly, no sane officer would order his men to fire before he got out of the way. In any event, the initial British volley hurt no one. It could have been a warning volley ordered by Pitcairn or one of his mounted officers. Perhaps also the soldiers aimed with deadly intent without orders, but shot high due to nerves. After all, they were not seasoned veteran troops. As at least one historian pointed out, the last action any of the British troops were involved in had occurred over 12 years earlier.[20] Many of the British troops, especially the younger men, had never seen combat.

Following the first apparently harmless volley, the British soldiers opened fire as individuals. Most of the Americans fled from the Common under this random fire, but several thought the British were firing blank charges and remained in ranks. As they retreated, a few Americans turned quickly and fired hastily aimed shots at the British, whose lines were all but obscured by the smoke from their firing. Perhaps one of these quickly aimed shots hit Johnson in the leg. According to Ensign Lister, Johnson of the 10th Regiment was the only British soldier wounded on Lexington Common.[21] In any event, the random British fire which followed the initial volley was fired with deadly intent and took a grim toll of the militiamen remaining on the Common.

After discharging their muskets, the high-spirited British soldiers advanced quickly over the ground the Lexington Militia had recently vacated. At least one wounded American, Jonas Parker, was run through with the bayonet as he struggled on the ground to reload his musket. Earlier in ranks, Parker, according to Sergeant William Munroe, had placed his balls and flint in his hat which was on the ground and vowed that he would not run from the British. He was as good as his word.[22]

---

[20] Ibid., "The British Soldiers," p. 9.

[21] Jeremy Lister, Concord Fight, Harvard University Press, Cambridge, 1931, "Narrative of Ensign Jeremy Lister," p. 24.

[22] Phinney, "William Munroe's March 7, 1825, Affidavit," p. 34.

Once the British moved forward with the bayonet, it did not take them long to clear the Common of living militiamen. The Lexington men, for the most part, had withdrawn beyond effective musket range, and had taken up positions in the woods and behind stone walls or other cover. From these positions, they continued a sporadic interchange of fire with the British which was ineffective on both sides due to the long distance separating the combatants. Gradually, this fire died out, as Lt. Col. Smith arrived on the Common with the main body. Smith, assisted by Pitcairn and other officers, soon restored order, but not without difficulty as the spirit of the soldiers was running high.

It should be mentioned that Major Edward Mitchell of the 5th Regiment may have played an aggressive role in the Lexington Common affair. Richard Pope, who was probably a private or noncommissioned officer in the 47th Regiment, wrote a little book entitled Richard Pope's Book from Notes. In this book, Pope claims that upon the rebels breaking their lines following the British fire, Mitchell and seven or eight officers charged them. This, of course, is barrack's hearsay as Pope marched with Lord Percy and was not present on Lexington Common during the fighting that took place there.[23] Still, it is easy to imagine the hot-tempered Mitchell assuming the role of the angry belligerent on Lexington Common. Perhaps he was the saber-waving officer, often mistaken for Pitcairn, who, according to American accounts, gave the order to fire. This writer feels that in the excitement it is possible that conflicting orders may have been given to the British soldiers prior to and during the firing on Lexington Common, and that Mitchell, or some overzealous junior officer, may have played a larger role in the tragedy than history will record.

In any case, following Smith's arrival on the scene, order was eventually restored and the British were reformed for their march to Concord. Before he gave the order to march, Smith had insured that the men who had fired on the Common had

---

[23] Kehoe, The British Soldiers, "Richard Pope's Book," pp. 156-157.

replaced the cartridges they had taken from their cartridge boxes. He clearly expected trouble ahead, but was determined to carry out the orders Gage had given him. He knew, of course, that any chance he had of surprising the guardians of the Province's military stores in Concord had been lost.

Rev. Jonas Clarke recorded that before the British left Lexington they fired a volley and gave three huzzahs of victory. Eight Americans were left dead behind them. Only three or four bodies were found in the area where the Lexington lines were formed. Asahel Porter, who had been taken prisoner by the British during their march to Lexington, was shot to death shortly after the British released him. His body was found near a stone wall about 20 rods east of the Common. The bodies of Samuel Hadley and John Brown were found off the Common. Caleb Harrington was felled near the Meeting House where he had gone to replenish his powder supply. According to an old Lexington tradition, Jonathan Harrington, who received a mortal wound on the Common, managed to drag himself to the doorstep of his nearby home where he died at the feet of his horror-stricken wife.[24] According to the narrative of the Lexington minister, Jonas Clarke, ten Americans were also wounded in the morning action on and near Lexington Common.[25] The British had one man, Johnson, wounded in the thigh, and possibly another man, according to one account, slightly wounded in the hand. Both were able to continue on with the troops to Concord. Major Pitcairn's horse was also hit twice during the action.

From the available evidence, it is uncertain as to which side fired first on Lexington Common. There are also other areas concerning the Lexington affair that we would like to know more about. For example, it is difficult for this writer to understand the rational basis behind the decision to keep Captain Parker and his

---

[24] Allen French, The Day of Concord and Lexington, Little Brown, Boston, 1925, p. 143.

[25] Rev. Ezra Ripley, A History of the Fight at Concord, Allen and Atwell, Concord, 1827, "Anniversary Sermon of the Rev. Jonas Clarke, April 19, 1776," p. 47.

company in Lexington. Once Hancock and Adams had been warned, it would seem that the logical thing to have done would have been to send the Lexington Militia to Concord. In Concord, Parker's men could have provided valuable assistance in guarding the vital military stores of the Province. After all, there was nothing in Lexington to interest the British, once Revere had alerted Hancock and Adams. Were the Lexington town officials, in consultation with other influential townsmen, solely responsible for the decision to keep Parker in Lexington or were there other factors involved? For example, what role, if any, did John Hancock and Samuel Adams play in the decision? History is silent on this question.

It is also hard to understand the reasoning behind the choice of Lexington Common as an area to deploy the Lexington Militia prior to the confrontation with the British. The flat, open ground of the Common, after all, provided Captain Parker's small force with no cover. It is difficult to believe that Parker would have chosen such a poor defensive position on his own. Perhaps he was influenced by other leading persons that were present. Doubtless he hoped that orders would come from his regimental colonel that would relieve him of the decision. No orders came, however, and Captain Parker was left with an inadequate force in a poor location to confront professional soldiers who greatly outnumbered him.

Historian John Galvin, in his book The Minute Men, pointed out another factor, which may have influenced the decision to place Parker and his men on the Common that fateful morning. Earlier on February 26, Colonel Alexander Leslie of the 64th Regiment was turned back at Salem's North Bridge by the appearance of armed Essex County militiamen. At other times during the past winter, the British had marched within firing range of armed militia units in the towns near Boston, but had not fired. There was a strong belief held by patriot leaders at the time that the British would not fire on the militia unless fired on first. Thinking along those lines, Captain Parker, who perhaps was influenced by others present, deployed his troops in a parade ground rather than battle formation in hope, perhaps, that the British would turn back at the sight of his company.

The above theory appears logical, but it is not supported by Captain Parker's own deposition in which the Lexington Captain plainly stated that after consultation he concluded "not to be discovered, nor meddle" with the British troops. Of course, this meeting occurred shortly after the Lexington men mustered for the first alarm and Parker's early decision may have been altered by 5 a.m. by the influence of others present. In fact, there is written testimony that Parker ordered his men to stand firm before he countermanded that order with his final order to disperse.

Another theory, quite Machiavellian in tone, is sometimes heard concerning the Lexington Common fighting. According to this theory, Samuel Adams influenced Parker to stand where he did in hopes that a clash of arms would occur and the war would begin. Adherents of this interesting theory usually quote the traditional words credited to Adams upon his notification of the fight on Lexington Common, "Oh what a glorious morning." There is, to my knowledge, no documentation to support the view that Samuel Adams directly manipulated the confrontation on Lexington Common.

Due to the unfavorable circumstances in which they were deployed, the end result which befell the Lexington Militia Company was entirely predictable. Not only was the casualty rate of the men who made the second muster extremely high, but they failed to inflict any meaningful damage on the British. For sheer determination against impossible odds, the individual courage of Jonas Parker stands out. It should be also noted, that despite their resounding loss on Lexington Common, the Lexington men were not finished, as events that occurred later in the day would prove.

The British behavior, on the other hand, will not stand as a model for army discipline. It is easy to blame the common soldier for his lack of order, but clearly the fifty-three-year-old Marine Major, John Pitcairn, lost temporary control of his men. While he is probably not the arch-villain earlier American historians made him out to be, he certainly must accept the responsibility for letting his troops get out of hand. In his defense, as John Galvin pointed out, Pitcairn was not in command of his accustomed marines. Moreover, the force he commanded on Lexington Common consisted of six companies of Light Infantry normally attached to six different regiments. In short, he commanded an unfamiliar detachment not used to working under his direction.

Of the British soldiers, it can be said that in spite of their temporary disorder, they acted in high spirit and displayed an aggressive desire to close with the enemy. It should be noted that relations between the British soldiers and the people of Boston were bad at that time. Perhaps, many of the men under Pitcairn viewed the situation on Lexington Common as a good opportunity to vent their frustration on the "Yankees," who they felt were the cause of much of their present misfortunes. In any event, their lack of order was not consistent with the image of the cool, professional soldier and was also a reflection on their officers and the ad hoc nature of their organization. Of Lt. Col. Frances Smith, it can be said to his everlasting credit that he restored order to the scene as quickly as possible, and prevented further needless bloodshed.

Of the citizens of Lexington, it can be said that despite the carnage that had been done to her sons by the British, the townsmen treated all prisoners that fell into their hands later that day in a humane fashion. Two British stragglers were, in fact, captured shortly after the British left Lexington by citizens of that town. On a march involving about 700 men, there is usually a number that can't keep up, and sometimes a few who separate on purpose.

In summary, the first clash of arms between the British Regulars and the organized Colonial Militia occurred on Lexington Common about 5 a.m. on April 19, 1775. It is not certain which side fired the first shot in this skirmish in which eight Americans were killed and ten wounded. One or two British enlisted men were also wounded along with Major Pitcairn's horse. The Americans who died on Lexington

Common were the first fatalities of the war that resulted in the independence of the United States. Last, but not least, the name of Lexington would serve as a rallying cry far beyond the borders of the town in the months to come.

3 - CONCORD

As the reader of Chapter 2 will recall, the British fired a victory salute and gave three huzzahs before they left the scene of their carnage on Lexington Common. As they marched toward Concord, the young soldiers among them must have felt proud and happy to have survived their first combat. The older officers and veterans, however, were probably more apprehensive, as they were deep in "rebel" territory and had lost the vital element of surprise.

The march through the town of Lincoln was fairly uneventful and would probably go unnoticed in the pages of history except for a description of the British column attributed to Mary Hartwell and printed in Abram English Brown's book, <u>Beneath Old Roof Trees</u> which was published in 1896. According to Brown, Mary Hartwell, told her grandchildren the following story concerning the appearance of the British troops as they passed on the road near Samuel Hartwell's house in Lincoln:

"The Army of the King was coming up in fine order, their red coats were brilliant, and their bayonets glistening in the sunlight made a fine

appearance; but I knew what all that meant, and I feared that I should never see your grandfather again."[1]

By "your grandfather", Mrs. Hartwell, of course, referred to her husband, Sergeant Samuel Hartwell of the Lincoln minute men. Historian Brown, like historian Frank Hersey, had received the above account from nineteenth century conversations he conducted with the grandsons of Mary Hartwell. The above description should be considered as family tradition rather than well-documented history. This writer has carefully compared the accounts of Brown and Hersey attributed to Mary Hartwell and has noted some significant differences in detail.

In any case, Mrs. Hartwell's statement concerning the "fine order" of the British soldiers coincides with the view of their commander, Lt. Col. Francis Smith. In his October 8, 1775, letter to R. Donkin, Smith made the following observation concerning his march to Concord:

"Marched on to Concord without firing a shot, tho' two were fired at us from the woods, and in all respects with as much good order as ever troops observed in Britain or any other friendly country."[2]

The shots Smith thought were fired at his soldiers on the march to Concord may have been fired in warning, or shots fired outside of effective musket range. Smith was obviously apprehensive as he proceeded to Concord, because he saw militiamen in the woods.[3] They didn't attack him in force, however, and nothing really noteworthy occurred along the march until the British reached Meriam's Corner in Concord.

---

[1] Abram English Brown, <u>Beneath Old Roof Trees</u>, Lee and Shepherd Publishers, Boston, 1896, p. 320.

[2] Vincent J. R. Kehoe, <u>We Were There: The British Soldiers</u>, "Letter from Lt. Col. Smith to R. Donkin," p. 75, Chelmsford, Massachusetts, 1973.

[3] Ibid., "Report of Lt. Col. Smith to General Gage."

Concord, of course, had been aware of the British approach, since young Dr. Prescott had rode into town some time after one o'clock. Shortly after the alarm bell sounded, the town's militia began to assemble near the town center. According to Thaddeus Blood, a member of Captain Nathan Barrett's militia company, his company drew their ammunition from a supply in the court house and paraded near the meeting house. He estimated the strength of his company at 60 to 70 men.[4]

The militia company Thaddeus Blood served in was only one of five military units raised in the Town of Concord. In addition to two minute companies under the commands of Captains David Brown and Charles Miles, there were two militia companies under the commands of Captains George Minot and Nathan Barrett.[5] A fifth company, referred to as the Alarm Company, had also been formed in Concord. The ranks of this company were filled with the older men of the town.

According to Coburn's muster rolls, the minute companies of Captains David Brown and Charles Miles contained 52 men each.[6] To the knowledge of this writer, no rolls of the two militia companies or the Alarm Company exist. In fact, Coburn in his search of the Commonwealth of Massachusetts Archives could find no official rolls for any of the Concord Companies, as the Town of Concord apparently filed no claims for the service of her men on April 19, 1775. The two minute company rolls Coburn printed were obtained from Tolman's Concord Minute Men and not from the State's official archives.

It is possible, however, to provide a pretty close estimate of the strength of Concord's militia companies from the account of Thaddeus Blood. According to Blood, Captain Barrett's militia

[4] Thaddeus Blood, "Thaddeus Blood's Account of April 19, 1775," p. 1, Concord Free Library, Concord, Massachusetts.

[5] Frank Warren Coburn, The Battle of April 19, 1775 in Lexington, Concord, Lincoln, Arlington, Cambridge, Somerville and Charlestown, Massachusetts, F. L. Coburn & Co., Printers, Boston, 1912, pp. 8-10.

[6] Ibid.

company originally contained 100 or more men, but only 60 or 70 paraded in the early evening hours of April 19th because about 30 joined the minute companies or were sent to guard the cannon that were transported to the woods. It is not certain, but not unlikely, that Concord's other militia company under Captain George Minot contained a similar number of men. In his account, Blood estimated the Concord men under arms prior to their march to Meriam's Corner as not less than 200 men.[7] Blood doubtless excluded the "gray heads" in the Alarm Company from his estimate. This writer has seen no documentation concerning the strength of the Alarm Company. Due to the age of its members, the Alarm Company was better suited for deployment in town as guardians of the supplies than for duty involving fast marches.

The Committee of the First Provincial Congress that had established the minute men in the preceding fall had recommended that each minute company contain fifty privates. However, in practice, as Coburn's rolls indicate, the strength of the minute companies that were actually established varied both in numbers and composition of officers and noncommissioned officers. A breakdown of Captain David Brown's Concord Minute Man Company shows the following organization:

1 Captain
2 Lieutenants
3 Sergeants
4 Corporals
1 Fifer
41 Privates

On the other hand, Captain Charles Mile's Concord Minute Man Company shows a slightly different organization which is listed by Coburn as follows:

1 Captain

---

[7] Blood, p. 1.

2 Lieutenants
4 Sergeants
1 Drummer
1 Fifer
3 Corporals
40 Privates[8]

The larger Lincoln Minute Man Company under Captain William Smith contained 62 officers and men. The organization of Captain Smith's minute company is listed in Coburn's rolls as follows:

1 Captain
1 Lieutenant
1 Second Lieutenant
4 Sergeants
4 Corporals
2 Fifers
1 Drummer
48 Privates[9]

The reader must remember that with the exception of the Concord rolls, which are unofficial, Coburn's rolls reflect only the men who actually mustered and claimed compensation as a result of their service on April 19, 1775. For the most part, Coburn's rolls also exclude those killed on April 19.

In April of 1775, there were two regiments, one of militia and one of minute men in the Concord area. Colonel James Barrett of Concord commanded the militia regiment, while Lt. Col. Ezekiel Howe of Sudbury was second in command. The minute man regiment was under the command of Colonel Abijah Pierce of Lincoln, who had as his second in command Lt. Col. Thomas Nixon of Framingham. In addition, Pierce's minute man

[8] Coburn, pp. 8-10.

[9] Ibid., pp. 13-14.

regiment had John Buttrick of Concord as Major and Jacob Miller of Holliston as Second Major. Coburn provides us with the following breakdown of these regiments:

Militia Regiment
Colonel James Barrett of Concord
Lt. Col. Ezekiel Howe of Sudbury
Captain Nathan Barrett of Concord
Captain George Minot of Concord
Captain Joseph Robbins of Acton
Captain John Moore of Bedford
Captain Samuel Farrar of Lincoln
Captain Moses Stone of Sudbury
Captain Aaron Haynes of Sudbury

Minute Man Regiment
Colonel Abijah Pierce of Lincoln
Lt. Col. Thomas Nixon of Framingham
Major John Buttrick of Concord
Second Major Jacob Miller of Holliston
Adjutant Thomas Hurd of East Sudbury
Captain David Brown of Concord
Captain Charles Miles of Concord
Captain Isaac Davis of Acton
Captain William Smith of Lincoln
Captain Jonathan Wilson of Bedford
Captain John Nixon of Sudbury[10]

It should be noted that the reorganization of the Massachusetts militia force had not been completed by the spring of 1775, and there was some confusion, especially in regard to the formation of the minute man companies and the selection of new officers. One newly selected field officer of minute men, Colonel Abijah Pierce of Lincoln, did not even have

---

[10] Ibid., pp. 7-8.

a weapon when he turned out on April 19. Many officers also lacked formal commissions until after April 19, 1775.

Following Dr. Prescott's alarm and the first muster of militia forces in Concord, the Concord men were dismissed and, like the Lexington company, they were ordered to muster again at the beat of a drum. Unlike the Lexington company, however, the Concord men did not go to their homes. Instead, they helped in removing some of the Provincial military stores that remained in Concord. Colonel James Barrett had been engaged in this activity since the preceding day. According to Lemuel Shattuck, four of the Province's cannon were removed to Stow and six were carried to other parts of the town. Others were concealed under hay, straw, manure, and so forth. Some of the military supplies were hauled to Acton and other towns, while other stores were concealed in private buildings in Concord and in the town's woods.[11]

As Colonel Barrett was engaged in seeing that the Province's military stores were properly secured, it was probably Major John Buttrick who ordered Reuben Brown on a scouting mission down the road toward Lexington. The mounted Brown arrived within sight of Lexington Common in time to see the British troops firing at the Lexington Militia. The cautious Brown did not stay to ascertain the results of the firing. Instead, wheeling his horse around, Brown reversed direction and sped back to Concord. Upon reporting his alarming news to Major Buttrick, the Concord major asked Brown if the British were firing ball. According to tradition Brown replied, "I do not know, but think it probable."[12]

Thanks to Brown's report, the Concord leaders knew where the British had been about 5 a.m. They could also surmise that the purpose of the British mission was to capture or destroy the Provincial military stores, which were now scattered in numerous

---

[11] Lemuel Shattuck, <u>History of Concord</u>, Russell, Odiorne and Company, Boston, 1835, p. 104.

[12] Ibid., pp. 103-104.

locations in various towns. However, it was possible that the British had turned back after the firing on Lexington Common. Clearly, further reconnaissance down the road to Lexington was needed.

The strength of the forces in Concord had been enhanced about four o'clock or so by the arrival of two companies from neighboring Lincoln. According to Thaddeus Blood, Captain William Smith commanded the minute man company, while Captain Abijah Pierce served as the militia companies' captain. Blood's account refers to Pierce as "afterwards Colonel." There is some doubt as to Pierce's exact function on April 19, 1775. This writer holds the view that Pierce might have been unsure of his field officer status and functioned only as a captain on April 19, 1775. According to Blood, none of the Provincial officers, except some who had been previously appointed by the Crown, held commissions on April 19, 1775.[13]

According to Blood, the minute and militiamen were then formed with the minute men on the right and Captain Nathan Barrett's militia company on the left. Blood says they were then marched in order to the end of Meriam's Hill where they spotted the British coming down Brook's Hill. Upon sight of the British, according to Blood's account, the Provincials then retreated back over the hill.[14]

Amos Barrett, writing some fifty years after the event, also provides us with an interesting view of this short march. Barrett's spelling is a bit irregular but the incident left a lasting impression on his mind:

"We marched down toward L. about a mild or mild half and we see them acoming, we halted and stayd till they got within about 100 rods then

---

[13] Blood, p. 1.

[14] Ibid.

we was orded to about face and marched before them with our drums and fifes agoing and also the B. We had grand musick."[15]

Barrett, who Coburn lists as a corporal in Captain David Brown's minute company, left the impression that his company marched up the road until they saw the British and then about faced and marched back to Concord Center in front of the British. On the other hand, Blood, the militiaman in Captain Barrett's company, clearly stated that his company retreated back over the hill.

The early nineteenth century historian Shattuck provided little detail on the short reconnaissance march of the Concord and Lincoln men. Concord historian Allen French wrote that "The Lincoln men, then, with the two Concord minute companies (some members being probably absent saving the stores) marched down the Lexington Road."[16] It is odd that French did not include the militia company of Captain Nathan Barrett with those who marched down the road as he was aware of the account of Thaddeus Blood.

The twentieth century historian and professional army officer, Major John. R. Galvin, U.S.A., wrote that Captain Brown's minute company marched down the road, while the two Concord militia companies paralleled them along the long ridge which runs along the northerly side of the road from Concord Center to Meriam's Corner.[17] Contemporary British accounts mention this ridge and the armed colonials they saw on it as the British column approached Concord. The British accounts are strangely silent, however, concerning armed colonials in the road ahead of them.

[15] Allen French, Ed., The Concord Fight, "An Account by Amos Barrett," Thomas Todd, Co., Boston, 1924, p. 12.

[16] Allen French, The Day of Concord and Lexington, Little Brown, Boston, 1925, p. 156.

[17] John R. Galvin, The Minute Men, Hawthorn Books, Inc., New York, 1967, p. 148.

In view of the evidence, as incomplete as it is, it is probably safe to say that a force of from perhaps 150 to 200 men proceeded toward Lexington around 7 a.m. on the morning of April 19, 1775. Perhaps they all started down the road, but at some point, at least one Concord militia company (Barrett's) moved on to the top of the long ridge on the north side of the road to Lexington. The militiamen on the ridge provided flank protection for at least one minute company (Brown's) on the road below. The Provincial force proceeded no farther eastward than Meriam's Corner in Concord about a mile from the meeting house. Upon sighting the British coming down the hill, they retreated back to Concord Center. Some withdrew along the top of the ridge in front of the Light Infantry who had been sent up to the ridge to dislodge them, and others returned on the road below in front of the British main body.

It should be pointed out that not all the Provincials who gathered in Concord on that bright April morning marched with the reconnaissance force to Meriam's Corner. The old men of Concord's Alarm Company, for example, were ordered up the steep ridge opposite the Meeting House where they were stationed until joined by the withdrawing reconnaissance force. A liberty pole had been erected not far from the position the Alarm Company occupied on the ridge.

As mentioned earlier, the British as they came down the long decline leading to Meriam's Corner, noticed an armed colonial force on the ridge to the right of the road. Lt. John Barker of the 4th regiment provides us with the following information:

"We met no interruption 'till within a mile or two of the Town, where the country people had occupied a hill which commanded the road; the Light Infantry were ordered away to the right and ascended the height in one line, upon which the Yankies quitted it without firing, which they did likewise for one or two more successively. They then crossed the river beyond the town and we marched into the town after taking possession of a hill with a Liberty Pole on it and a flag flying which was cut down; the Yankies had that hill

but left it to us; we expected they would have made a stand there, but they did not chuse it."[18]

In short, the Provincials drew back along the ridge until they reached a position near the Liberty Pole where the Alarm Company was posted. Taking the Alarm Company with them, the colonial force further withdrew to a second ridge which ran parallel to the road leading to the Rev. William Emerson's parsonage. According to the Rev. Emerson, some of the outnumbered Provincials were for making a stand against the larger British force, but "other more prudent thought best to retreat till our strength should be equal to the enemy's, by recruits from neighboring towns that were continually coming to our assistance."[19]

It should be noted that according to Concord tradition, the Rev. William Emerson was one of the most vocal Concordians in favor of a stand against the British. It was probably at this point on the second ridge that Colonel James Barrett exerted his influence and authority. Barrett, who had been previously occupied with the security of the Provincial military stores, cautioned the colonials against careless actions that would needlessly expose themselves. According to the Rev. Ezra Ripley, Barrett ordered his Provincials to

"march over the North Bridge, and take a position on a hill about one mile to the north of the meeting house, and there to wait for accessions to their numbers, and for further orders."[20]

---

[18] Elizabeth Ellery Dana, Editor, The British in Boston," Lt. John Barker's Diary," Harvard University Press, Cambridge, 1924, pp. 32-33.

[19] Rev. William Emerson, "Reverend William Emerson's Diary: Entry for April 19, 1775," p. 2, Minute Man National Historical Park, Historical Files, Concord, Massachusetts.

[20] Reverend Ezra Ripley, D.D., A History of the Fight at Concord on the 19th of April, 1775, Allen & Atwill, Concord, Massachusetts, 1827, p. 16.

Upon reaching the Liberty Pole, which was probably on the ridge in back of Reuben Brown's house, the British soldiers cut it down. While the Light Infantry had been moving along the ridge, the main body, including the grenadiers, approached Concord by the road below. In the brilliant sunshine of the morning, they must have been a splendid sight to behold. They probably arrived in Concord before 8 a.m.

The Light Infantry, which had so effectively cleared the ridge of any possible opposition, were now deployed on a different mission. Captain Mundy Pole with one detachment was sent to the South Bridge. His orders were to secure the bridge and destroy any military stores in the vicinity.

Lt. Col. Smith also detached a force of Light Infantry with the dual mission of destroying military stores at Colonel James Barrett's farm and securing Concord's North Bridge. For this purpose, Smith assigned Captain Lawrence Parsons of the 10th Regiment of Foot with six companies of Light Infantry.

In addition to the military stores at Colonel Barrett's farm and the South Bridge area, Provincial supplies were stored at various locations in Concord, which included the central part of the town. The duty of locating and destroying these centrally located supplies fell mainly to the grenadiers of Smith's detachment. Lt. Col. Smith, Major Pitcairn, and the other officers not deployed with the Light Infantry companies remained in Concord Center to direct the search for the concealed supplies in their vicinity.

Shortly after Colonel Barrett cautioned his men on the ridge east of the Concord River, he ordered them to make an orderly withdrawal to the high ground to the west of the river where they could wait for reinforcements. The wisdom of this Fabian tactic cannot be questioned, as Barrett's minute and militia forces were too weak to oppose the British at that point. As the Provincial force withdrew over the North Bridge, the Light Infantry companies of Captain Parsons marched close behind them. According to both the Lincoln and Concord depositions, the British detachment consisted of about 200 men.[21] (If the estimate

---

[21] Shattuck, "Depositions of 24 Lincoln and Concord Men, April 23, 1775," pp. 347-348.

of 200 British is accurate, and Parsons' detachment contained six companies, then the average strength of each company was about 33 men. This figure is consistent with other estimates of British company strength based on different documentation.)

According to the Lincoln and Concord depositions, the British left about half of their 200 men at the North Bridge and proceeded on to Colonel Barrett's with the rest. The men Captain Parsons left at the North Bridge were under the command of Captain Walter Sloan Laurie of the 43rd Regiment of Foot. According to Laurie's April 26, 1775 report to General Gage, Parsons stationed him and his company of the 43rd regiment at the bridge along with a company from the 5th regiment.[22] Parsons passed west of the bridge with the other four Light Infantry companies, but he only took the 38th and 52nd companies with him to Barrett's. On the higher ground west of the Concord River, he left a company from the 4th regiment and a company from the 10th regiment.[23]

The 4th regiment company was commanded by Lt. Edward Gould while the 10th regiment company was commanded by Lt. Waldron Kelly. According to Lt. Sutherland's account, the height the British were posted on was not more that 300 yards from the bridge. The two companies were not together, however, as Lt. Barker's diary account states that "1 of these companies, was left at the bridge, another on a hill some distance from it, and another on a hill 1/4 of a mile from that..."[24]

The narrative account of Ensign Jeremy Lister of His Majesty's 10th Regiment of Foot also mentions that the 4th and 10th regiment companies were posted on two different hills in

---

[22] Allen French, General Gage's Informers, "Captain Walter S. Laurie's Report to General Gage, April 26, 1775," p. 95, The University of Michigan Press, Ann Arbor, 1932.

[23] Ibid., "Letter of Lt. Wm. Sutherland to General Gage's Secretary, April 27, 1775," pp. 87-88.

[24] Dana, "Lt. John Barker's Diary Account," p. 33.

order to command the road Captain Parsons took to Colonel Barrett's farm.[25]

Ensign DeBerniere, an officer noted for his attention to detail, noted that the companies left to protect the bridge were not close together, "but situated so as to be able to support each other."[26]

The most specific American account I have seen concerning the location of the British companies is that of the Concord Militiaman Thaddeus Blood. According to Blood, some of the British "tarried near the bridge, some of them to Capt. David Brown's and some Mr. Ephm Buttrick where Colonel Jonas Buttrick now lives."[27]

Blood probably viewed this disposition of British forces from Punkatasset Hill, as he stated that colonials marched to that location after crossing the bridge.

The only known contemporary map showing the deployment of forces in Concord on April 19, 1775 is the so-called Mackenzie Map, which Allen French reprinted in the book he entitled A British Fusilier in Revolutionary Boston. This book is a reprint of the diary Lt. Frederick Mackenzie, Adjutant of the Royal Welch Fusiliers, maintained while he was in Boston.[28] Mackenzie, assigned to the 23rd regiment, was not at the scene of the Concord fighting as he came out with Lord Percy's Brigade. Therefore, he may not have drawn the map that was posted in his diary. French thought that Ensign DeBerniere might have drawn the map but that is speculation. DeBerniere, of course, served as guide to Captain Parsons on the expedition to Colonel Barrett's farm. The Ensign would have observed the

---

[25] Jeremy Lister, Concord Fight, "Narrative of Ensign Jeremy Lister," pp. 24-25, Harvard University Press, Cambridge, 1931.

[26] Kehoe, The British Soldiers, "Ensign DeBerniere' s Report to General Gage," p. 121.

[27] Blood, p. 2.

[28] Allen French, Ed., A British Fusilier in Revolutionary Boston, Harvard University Press, Cambridge, 1926, p. 78.

positions where Captain Parsons initially posted the 4th and 10th regiment companies, but they might have adjusted their positions after Parsons' detachment left for Barrett's.

In any case, the Mackenzie Map shows the 10th regiment company positioned west of the river, on top of a hill just east of a man-made structure. It is probably one of the Buttrick houses, but as other eighteenth century homes in the area are not indicated on the map, it is uncertain which Buttrick structure the 10th is posted near. It is, however, just south of the position on the map indicating the location of the American disposition just prior to their advance toward the bridge and Concord Center (muster field).

The position of the 4th regiment company on the Mackenzie Map is drawn in on what appears to be a southwestern slope west of the 10th regiment company's positions. It is also nearer to the road to Colonel Barrett's and appears to be on Captain David Brown's higher land.

The Mackenzie Map also shows the position of Captain Laurie's 43rd regiment company on the east side of the bridge. We know, of course, from various accounts, that Captain Laurie's company was on the west side of the bridge prior to the colonial advance on Concord, and that he fell back with his own and the 4th and 10th companies for his brief unsuccessful defense of the bridge. The point is, the Mackenzie map, if drawn by DeBerniere, may represent the initial, but not the final positions the three British companies were deployed in prior to their withdrawal to the east side of the North Bridge.

Additional information concerning the position of Gould's 4th regiment company is provided in Captain Laurie's April 26, 1775 report to General Gage. In this report, Laurie noted that upon the approach of the colonials, the Light Company of the 4th regiment retreated to join his company at the bridge. Laurie went to add "By this time the body of the country people, arrived on the heights, which the company of the 4th Regt. had occupied, and there drew up with shouldered arms..."[29]

---

[29] French, General Gage's Informers, "Captain Laurie's Report to General Gage," p. 97.

In view of the evidence, it would appear that the 4th regiment company was posted on the high land of Captain David Brown in what we now call the "Muster Field." From this position it could provide security to the north, where the colonials were gathering, and also keep the road to Colonel Barrett's under surveillance. On the other hand, the 10th regiment company was probably posted east of the 4th near the Ephraim Buttrick house where it could also provide security to the north, as well as surveillance of Groton Road. From their separate positions, both companies could fall back and support Laurie at the bridge if he needed them.

As mentioned earlier, Captain Parsons had left a Light Company from the 5th regiment with Laurie's 43rd at the bridge. The 5th regiment company did not stay long with Captain Laurie. According to Laurie's report to General Gage,

"In less than a half an hour the Light Company of the 23rd Regt. with Captn Browne of the 52d and Lieut. Grant of the Artillery, came past me in a chaise to join Captn Parsons, who immediately sent an order to the 5th Company to advance, leaving my company at the bridge."[30]

Doubtless Captain Parsons felt the need for additional reinforcements at Barrett's farm as he called for the 5th regiment company after the 23rd regiment company had arrived. Captain Brown of the 52nd regiment had gone on, of course, to join his company that had earlier taken the lower road to Colonel Barrett's with Captain Parsons. The presence of Lt. Grant, an artillery officer, at Barrett's farm can be explained by the fact that the British hoped to find cannon concealed at Colonel Barrett's. Perhaps, if Grant thought the quality of the cannon was worthwhile, the British could bring them back. If powder and cannon balls were also found at Barrett's, Smith's force could have used the cannons, if necessary, to cover their withdrawal from Concord. In the very least, Grant was available to supervise the destruction of the cannon if any were found. In any event,

---

[30] Ibid., pp. 95-96.

Captain Parsons eventually had four companies with him at Colonel Barrett's farm. These companies were from the following regiments: 5th, 23rd, 38th and 52nd. In the meantime, Captain Laurie was at the North Bridge with the 43rd supported by the 4th and 10th regiment companies on the higher ground to the west of the Concord River.

At this point, the British force in Concord was roughly divided into four detachments. The main body of troops, including the grenadiers, remained in the village area with Lt. Col. Smith and Major Pitcairn, four Light Companies were at Colonel Barrett's under Parsons, three Light companies were in the North Bridge area, under Laurie, Gould, and Kelly, while a detachment under Captain Mundy Pole was at the South Bridge. But what about Colonel Barrett's Provincials?

After he had given the order to march over the North Bridge to the higher ground on the west side of the river, Colonel Barrett, according to Shattuck, rode off in the direction of his farm to insure that the military supplies there were safely concealed. The ranking officer present with the colonial force was once again the Regimental Major of Minute Men John Buttrick.

As the Provincials passed over the North Bridge to the west side, the two hundred or so British Light Infantrymen under Captain Parsons were close behind them. At that point, Major Buttrick must have wished to put some distance between his men and the six British companies. According to a tradition in the Hunt family, Buttrick led his force to Punkatasset Hill, which is located on what was then the Hunt farm.[31] Punkatasset Hill is located west of present day Monument Street and is roughly 3/4 of mile north of the North Bridge.

Normally, there would be no reason to doubt the Hunt family tradition that the colonials, or at least some of them, used Punkatasset Hill as a temporary position. The hill provided a good observation point, it was defensible, and from there Buttrick's force was in no immediate danger from Parsons' Light

---

[31] French, The Day of Concord and Lexington, p. 182 (footnote).

Infantry. According to Shattuck, however, Colonel Barrett had ordered his 150 men to march over the North Bridge and take up a position near what was then the homes of Ephraim and Willard Buttrick.[32]

There is also no reason to doubt Shattuck's statement as to the order left by Colonel Barrett. However, there is good reason to believe that Major Buttrick, seeing that he was closely followed by Parsons' Light companies, modified Barrett's order and withdrew his men further to the north. A glance at Mackenzie's Map, shows that two British companies (4th and 10th) took up positions that were very near to the area of the muster field where the Americans later formed. According to Lt. Sutherland's account, after posting two companies at the bridge, Captain Parsons marched to the top of the hill where the following disposition of colonials could be seen (remember Sutherland viewed this disposition from the high ground overlooking the North Bridge):

"The part of them formed in a meadow and the rest went still further off with the women and children and formed in another meadow on a rising ground, I saw more men in arms on a height that rose above the last mentioned party."[33]

From a close reading of Sutherland's account, it would appear that the colonials were in four temporary positions: a meadow, another meadow further off, a rising ground, and a hill above the rising ground. The latter two positions may have been Punkatasset Hill and its southwestern slope. Lt. Sutherland's account then, seems to support the Hunt family tradition that Punkatasset Hill was used as a temporary gathering place for colonial forces, or at least some of them. In any case, it is quite unlikely that Captain Parsons would have posted the two Light

---

[32] Shattuck, p. 106.

[33] Kehoe, The British Soldiers, "Letter of Lt. Wm. Sutherland to Sir Henry Clinton, April 26, 1775," p. 142.

Infantry companies (4th and 10th) as close as he did to the muster field area if a sizable force of colonials were positioned there. After all, the two British companies probably totaled less than 70 men and they were separated.

In view of the evidence, it is probably safe to say that Major Buttrick withdrew his forces no further than Punkatasset Hill, where they took up temporary positions on the hill and land below the hill in the direction of the North Bridge. Some of them escorted their women and children to another meadow even more secure. The women and children, who probably came from the area west of the bridge, may also explain in part why Major Buttrick wanted distance between himself and the British. In any event, Buttrick, although in a good position to wait for reinforcements, was too far north of Town to protect the military stores. Soon, however, his ranks would grow in both numbers and boldness, but that is getting ahead of the story.

In the meantime, the main British force in Concord continued their search for military supplies. Earlier, under the direction of Colonel James Barrett, the colonials had succeeded in concealing much of the military stores. Near the center of Town, however, the British did find about 60 barrels of flour and about 500 pounds of musket balls, which they threw in the Mill Pond and various wells. They also knocked the trunnions of three iron 24-pound cannon and burnt 16 new carriage wheels and a few barrels of wooden trenchers and spoons.[34] According to Amos Barrett's letter, some of the flour that was thrown into the Mill Pond was later recovered.[35] Apparently, the outer flour in the barrels swelled making the barrels waterproof.

In general, during their search for military stores in Concord, the British respected the persons and property of private citizens. They were careless, however, in their use of fire as will be seen later. During their occupation of Concord, they had many interactions with citizens of that town. The limited scope of this

---

[34] Shattuck, p. 107.

[35] French, The Concord Fight, "An Account by Amos Barrett," pp. 12-13.

report does not permit a retelling of the traditional stories related to these interesting encounters. This writer should refer the interested reader to such original accounts as that given by Martha Moulton and William Emerson. The reader should also consult such secondary source material as contained in the writings of the Rev. Ezra Ripley, Lemuel Shattuck, Allen French and, of course, that unexcelled repeater of local tradition, Ellen Chase. The latter writer's work is contained in three volumes entitled: The Beginnings of the American Revolution.

As the British force conducted their search for military stores, the Provincial force on and near Punkatasset Hill was reinforced by companies and individuals from neighboring towns. It was in this vicinity that the Bedford Company of Minute Men, led by Captain Jonathan Wilson, and the Bedford Militia Company, under the command of Captain John Moore, probably arrived. The Bedford Minute Company was understrength, as the rolls list only 28 men including its three officers. The roll of the Bedford Militia Company, on the other hand, shows a total of 47 officers and men.[36]

According to Bedford tradition, the men of that town marched under a banner which closely resembles the richly made cornets carried by English cavalry troops in the English Civil War of the mid-seventeenth century. Some historians believe that the flag was carried on the standard of the "Three County Troop," a cavalry company existing between 1659 and 1677 in Essex, Suffolk, and Middlesex Counties in Massachusetts. If this is the case, the flag could have been passed down from preceding generations to the 1775 Bedford minute and militia men. In any event, the flag shows the strong right arm of an armored warrior gripping a sword. Featured against a rich red background and trimmed in gold, the banner displays the Latin words:

"Vince Aut Morire"
(Conquer or Die)

---

[36] Coburn, pp. 11-12.

This writer has not found any contemporary accounts relating to the Bedford Flag. Apparently, the tradition was not widely known until 1836 when it was immortalized in Ralph Waldo Emerson's famous stanza from the "Concord Hymn."

> *"By the rude bridge which arched the flood,*
> *Their flag to April's breeze unfurled,*
> *Here once the embattled farmers stood,*
> *And fired the shot heard round the world."*

In any event, the two Bedford companies joined the ranks of the five Concord companies and two Lincoln companies in the Punkatasset Hill and Hunt farm area. The Hunt farm was connected through the Estabrook pastures with lanes leading to the roads from Acton and the Carlisle area. Individuals and small groups of men from such places as Carlisle, Littleton, Chelmsford, and Westford also arrived. Lt. Col. John Robinson came from the latter town in advance of his company, which arrived too late to participate in the North Bridge fighting. According to tradition, the Rev. Joseph Thaxter, who was then a candidate for the Westford pulpit, came along with pistols in his pockets.[37]

At what point Colonel Barrett rejoined his colonials is unclear. In any case, their ranks had swelled and they now enjoyed a numerical advantage over the British in the North Bridge area. It must have occurred to the colonial leaders that they were positioned too far from the town to either guard the military stores or to protect Concord Village. They might have realized also that only two British companies were positioned between them and the company at the North Bridge. In any event, they advanced towards the bridge in the direction of the area where Lt. Kelly's 10th regiment company and Lt. Gould's 4th regiment company were posted.

Little is known of the Provincial advance from the Hunt farm area to the area now known as the "muster field." The term,

---

[37] French, The Day of Concord and Lexington, p. 184.

"muster field," as historian Cynthia E. Kryston pointed out in her 1972 report of the same name, is a modern one. In 1775 the land where the colonials waited prior to their action at the North Bridge was probably on part of Captain David Brown's farm.[38]

Upon the approach of the colonials, the British 10th regiment company under Lt. Kelly fell back from its position near one of the Buttrick houses and joined the 4th regiment company, which was probably nearer the road to Colonel Barrett's farm on the southwestern slope of David Brown's land. Lt. Barker feared that the advancing colonials would cut the British companies from the bridge.[39] Ensign Jeremy Lister who was with Lt. Kelly's company described the British withdrawal to the bridge in the following manner:

"We had not been long in this situation when we saw a large body of men drawn up with the greatest regularity and approached us seemingly with an intent to attack, when Lt. Kelly who then commanded our company with myself thought it most proper to retire from our situation and join the 4th Company which we did, they still approached and in that force, that it was thought proper by the officers except myself to join the 43rd Company at Concord Bridge commanded by Captain Laurie."[40]

Lister's account shows that the 10th and 4th companies withdrew to the lower ground and combined with Captain Laurie's company of the 43rd regiment. Captain Laurie assumed command of the three companies and concentrated his detachment just west of the North Bridge. In this location he had little room to maneuver, as he was hemmed in by the Concord River on one side and a marshy meadow on the other. He was also concerned by the large force of colonials who were forming

---

[38] Kryston, Cynthia E., "The Muster Field: Historic Data," (unpublished report) Minute Man National Historical Park, Concord, Massachusetts, 1972, p. 9.

[39] Dana, "Lt. John Barker's Diary Account," p. 33.

[40] Lister, p. 25.

on the high ground overlooking his position. He, therefore, sent Lt. Robertson, of his own company, to Concord Center with the request that he be reinforced.[41]

The colonials in the meantime were forming in the pasture of David Brown west of the Ephraim and Willard Buttrick houses. According to Shattuck, Lt. Joseph Hosmer, acting as adjutant, formed the units as they arrived so that they faced the town with the minute men on the right and the militia on the left.[42] This formation made military sense, as a few short commands could quickly convert the formation to a column with the minute companies in the lead in case of trouble at the bridge or in town.

While the men waited in ranks facing the Town of Concord, a group of their officers and leading citizens debated their next move. Apparently, they were still uncertain as to whether or not anyone was killed at Lexington, even though that fighting had occurred at least four hours earlier. Their main concern, however, must have been for the safety of the Town of Concord and the military stores. They must have been concerned also because their minute and militia regiments were not fully mustered. For example, the companies from Sudbury and Acton had not yet arrived.

As the leaders continued their discussion, men from neighboring Acton, including about 38 men in Captain Isaac Davis's company arrived. Earlier in the morning, the thirty-year-old Davis and some of his men made cartridges in his home. His four children were at that time ill with the canker-rash and his last words to his wife Hannah were "Take good care of the children."[43] According to eyewitness Charles Handley's deposition, the Acton men marched at a fast pace to the music of a fife and drum as they took the road at Brown's Tavern, which

---

[41] Ibid., p. 26.

[42] Shattuck, p. 111.

[43] Josiah Adams, An Address Delivered at Acton July 21, 1835, J. T. Buckingham, Boston, 1835, "Deposition of the Wife of Capt. Davis," p. 47.

led to the high ground above the bridge. Handley was not sure of the tune the fife and drum were playing, but he thought it was the "White Cockade."[44]

Captain Davis positioned his company to the left of the already assembled formations of Concord minute men, as he had done a few weeks earlier at a regimental muster in Concord.[45] When Davis arrived, the Concord minute companies, which had been established earlier, were formed in the position of honor to the right as they had done in the earlier regimental muster in March.[46] Leaving his company, Captain Davis joined the group of officers that were consulting a few rods away from his company's position.

In the meantime, the British in Concord had lit fires in order to destroy such combustible items as wooden spoons, trenchers, and gun carriages. According to the petition of Martha Moulton on February 4, 1776 to the General Court of Massachusetts, the British were burning gun carriages when the nearby Court, or Town House as it was often called, caught fire. According to the seventy-one year old widow, she pleaded with four of five officers who were seated outside in chairs (probably in front of Wright's Tavern) to put out the fire. The officers at first appeared indifferent to Widow Moulton's pleadings, but after a while an order was given and the soldiers started to dump pails of water on the flames in the Town House.[47] In addition to the Town House fire and the gun carriage bonfire, the harness shop of Reuben Brown's also started to burn. There were other outside bonfires as well as those indicated above.

---

[44] Ibid., "Charles Handley's Deposition, Dec. 1, 1835," p. 47.

[45] Ibid., "Solomon Smith's Deposition, July 10, 1835," p. 45.

[46] Ibid., "Thomas Thorp's Deposition, July 10, 1835," p. 42.

[47] Richard Frothingham, History of the Siege of Boston and of the Battles, of Lexington, Concord and Bunker Hill, "Petition of Martha Moulton, Feb. 4, 1776," p. 370, Little, Brown and Company, Boston, 1896.

Whether the Town House accidentally caught fire from a spark from the nearby gun carriage bonfire or whether it was purposely set by the British is not clear from Martha Moulton's 1776 petition. However, writing some 50 years later, Amos Barrett stated in his unique spelling style:

> *"Thair was in the town house a number of intreaken tools witch they carried out and burnt them. At last they said it was better to burn them in the house and sot fire to them in the house, but our people begged them not to burn the house, and put it out. It wont long before it was set fire again but finally it warnt burnt."*[48]

The reader must remember, of course, that Amos Barrett was not in any position to see who set the fire, as he was standing on the high ground overlooking the Concord River with Captain David Brown's minute company. He must have received his knowledge of the subject later from others.

Historians Ripley, Shattuck, and Tolman are among those who believed the British deliberately set the Town House on fire, but they didn't provide documentation to support their view. George Tolman also wrote that the British set fire to Reuben Brown's harness shop.[49] In any case, neither structure was destroyed by the fire, as the flames were extinguished. The fire, however, caused smoke and this smoke was seen from the ranks of the watching colonials on the high ground overlooking the North Bridge.

According to Thaddeus Blood's account, it was about 9 o'clock when they first saw smoke rising from the court house fire. It must have caused grave concern in the ranks of the colonials, especially among the Concord men, who had loved ones and property in town. According to a Concord tradition repeated by Shattuck, Lt. Joseph Hosmer was so moved by the

---

[48] French, The Concord Fight, "An Account by Amos Barrett," p. 12.

[49] George Tolman, Events of April Nineteen, Concord Antiquarian Society, Concord, Massachusetts, p. 27.

sight of the smoke that he went to the gathering of officers and leading citizens and asked, "Will you let them burn the town down?"[50] Hosmer, who the town's leading Tory had once described as "the most dangerous man in Concord," was not the only officer willing to go to the town's defense.[51] Captain William Smith of the Lincoln minute men volunteered to dislodge the British from the bridge.[52] It was not, however, Smith who Major Buttrick chose to lead the advance to save the town. Even though Smith's company contained about 62 men, Major Buttrick selected the smaller 38-man minute company of Captain Isaac Davis of Acton. Why did the Regimental Major of Minute Men choose Davis' company?

To begin with Captain Davis was, like Smith, a young man of spirit and patriotic feelings. Closer to the point, however, Captain Smith's company, according to Amos Baker's 1850 deposition had no cartridge boxes and most importantly, only one bayonet in the whole company. According to Baker, Major Buttrick wanted only minute men with bayonets in the front of the column.[53] Therefore, the honor and danger of leading the advance was given to Captain Davis, who doubtless also volunteered for the dangerous assignment.

The decision to place minute men with bayonets in the lead was a good one. Suppose for example, Buttrick had sent Smith's Lincoln company to the front with only one bayonet. The British, seeing that the lead company had practically no bayonets, could have withheld their fire and blocked passage over the bridge with a solid wall of bayonets. In this situation, the Lincoln men would have been forced to shoot the British in order to get through their steel barrier. However, by putting the men with

---

[50] Shattuck, p. 111.

[51] French, The Day of Concord and Lexington, p. 160.

[52] Frothingham, "Statement of Major John Buttrick," p. 68.

[53] Vincent J. R. Kehoe, We Were There: The American Rebels, "Affidavit of Amos Baker, April 22, 1850," pp. 303-304.

bayonets in the lead, Buttrick greatly reduced the possibility that the British would try to stop him with a bayonet bluff. Buttrick had watched the two British companies withdraw from the high ground he now occupied. Perhaps, he thought the small force at the bridge would do the same.

Following the impromptu officer's conference, Captain Davis returned to face the men in the ranks of his Acton company. According to the affidavit of the Acton Minute Man Solomon Smith, Captain Davis drew his sword and said to his company, "I haven't a man that is afraid to go, and gave the word 'march'."[54] The Acton company then shifted its position from the left of the minute man line to the right of the Concord minute men, so it would be in a position to lead the advance toward Concord Center.

The final order to advance, of course, was the responsibility of the ranking officer present, Colonel James Barrett. The sixty-five year old Barrett had put in a hard night of riding back and forth to various places in order to insure that the Province's military stores were safely concealed. As a result of his involvement in this activity, he had spent much of the morning away from the two partial regiments that were now formed on the high ground overlooking the North Bridge. He was with them now, however, and the responsibility for what might occur next was squarely on his shoulders. He probably would have liked to wait for the arrival of more reinforcements to fill out the empty places in his two regiments, but the rising smoke from Concord made an advance imperative. He could see the 96 or so British in the North Bridge area and probably knew he faced 400 or so Regular troops in and around Concord Center. He knew also that when the British companies that went to his farm returned, he could easily be caught between two forces. He thought, perhaps, that Sudbury and companies from other regiments would soon arrive with much needed reinforcements. Come what may, he could delay no longer.

---

[54] Adams, p. 45.

Earlier the minute and militia men had loaded their weapons under the eyes of their captains. Amos Baker of Lincoln loaded his musket with two one-ounce balls with an appropriate amount of powder.[55] Some of the colonials had cartridge boxes. Others carried their powder in old-fashioned powder horns. While waiting in the muster field, many had replaced their flints in order to increase the reliability of their muskets. They did not know what to expect from the British, but they had obviously prepared for the worst.

Colonel Barrett could see that the colonial force was ready to march. He was concerned, however, that they might fire first and initiate a conflict with the smaller British force at the bridge. He, therefore, rode along the colonial line cautioning his men not to fire unless fired upon first.

The order to march was given and the Acton company, formed in double file, stepped off first with the other minute and militia companies following. In the lead was the Regimental Major of Minute Men, John Buttrick of Concord. Westford's Lt. Col. John Robinson, a member of Colonel Prescott's regiment, marched by Major Buttrick's side. Robinson had arrived in advance of his men. According to Concord tradition, Major Buttrick offered his command to his superior in rank, but Robinson wisely declined, as he didn't want to deprive the Concord Major of the command of the minute man regiment Buttrick was familiar with.[56] Captain Davis, at the head of his minute company, was also among the leaders of the colonial advance. Colonel Barrett remained mounted, and rode nearer the rear where he could exert his influence over the militia companies.

Historians have never determined the clear order of all the companies on the march to the bridge. According to Concord's Rev. Ezra Ripley, the Acton company under Captain Davis led, followed by the Concord minute companies of Captain David

---

[55] Kehoe, The American Rebels, "Affidavit of Amos Baker, April 22, 1850," p. 303.

[56] French, The Day of Concord and Lexington, p. 189-190.

Brown and Charles Miles. He records the Concord Militia Company under Captain Nathan Barrett as coming fourth, followed by the Lincoln and Bedford companies under Colonel Barrett's direction.[57]

Historian Lemuel Shattuck, however, presented an order of advance different from the view held by most historians. According to Shattuck, Captain Brown's Concord Minute Company originally was in front but was passed by Captain Davis' company, which then halted in front of the advancing column. According to Shattuck, Captain Brown marched his men along the north side of Davis' company until they were equally in front.[58] Shattuck's interesting contention, however, is not supported by the weight of existing evidence and tradition. For example, Amos Barrett, a Corporal in Captain David Brown's company, did not mention that his company was abreast of the Acton company. Barrett clearly stated, however, that Captain Davis marched first.

From the available documentation, it would appear that the companies had earlier lined up in the "Muster Field" with the minute companies to the right and the militia companies to the left. Normally, the minute companies would all have preceded the militia companies on the march to the bridge. It is, however, a documented fact that the Lincoln company was woefully lacking in bayonets and cartridge boxes. This may have been the reason it was probably preceded down the hill by the Concord Militia Company of Captain Nathan Barrett. The reader should note, however, that contemporary evidence relating to the number of bayonets in the Concord companies on April 19, 1775, is inadequate.

Except for Davis' company, which moved from the left of the Concord Minutemen to the right of them just prior to the advance, the available evidence indicates that the colonial minute and militia units began their advance from their right. The British

---

[57] Ripley, pp. 25-26.

[58] Shattuck, p. 111.

Lt. Sutherland, who had joined Captain Laurie at the bridge, plainly states, however, in his letter to General Gage's Secretary, that the colonials began their march "from their left."[59] Sutherland's remark appears to conflict with the weight of American evidence, until one considers the initial movement of Davis' company to the right of the line. The last-minute movement of the Acton men in the "Muster Field" may have given the British lieutenant the impression that the Provincial line was advancing from its left.

It appears that early historians focused most of their attention on the question of "who led the advance" and paid less attention to the order of companies following the leaders. From a close study of the extant evidence, however, it appears certain that the Acton minute men under Captain Davis led the Provincial advance. The two Concord minute companies under Captains Brown and Miles came next, followed by Captain Nathan Barrett's Concord Militia Company. The order of companies after that is uncertain. In general, the minute companies probably preceded the remaining militia companies with the exception of at least the Lincoln Minute Man Company, which was probably dropped back due to its lack of bayonets and cartridge boxes. The older men of the Concord Alarm Company probably brought up the rear.

The following four towns were represented during the march to the bridge with companies at or approaching full company organization: Acton, Concord, Bedford, and Lincoln. There were individuals and contingents from other neighboring towns also present. Estimates of the number of Americans who participated in that fateful march to the bridge vary from 300 to 1500. For example, the April 23, 1775 deposition of Bradbury Robinson, Samuel Spring, and Thaddeus Bancroft of Concord places the American force at 300.[60] On the other hand, the estimate of the

---

[59] French, General Gage's Informers, "Lt. Wm. Sutherland's Letter to General Gage's Secretary, April 27, 1775," p. 89.

[60] Shattuck, "Deposition of Bradbury Robinson, Samuel Spring, Thaddeus Bancroft and James Adams, April 23, 1775," p. 349.

British captain, Walter S. Laurie, places the strength of the colonials at "about 1500."[61] Laurie's estimate is, of course, too high. Laurie was not the first, or the last, officer in history to overestimate the strength of the enemy, especially in a losing situation. Another British officer, Lt. Gould, estimated the colonial force at about "three or four hundred."[62] The Rev. Ezra Ripley estimated the Provincial force at about 450, while historian Allen French wrote that the Provincial force was between 300 and 450 men.[63] This writer has studied Coburn's muster rolls, but as they do not provide figures for all the participating companies, they are not conclusive. Until additional evidence comes to light, this writer will have to go along with the figure of 450 as a rough estimate of the colonial strength on the march to the North Bridge.

Documentation relating to the colonial arms is also inadequate. In his 1850 deposition, Amos Baker said that the minute men were put in front because they were the only men that had bayonets. He also noted that he had the only bayonet in the Lincoln company, which also lacked cartridge boxes. The inference is that the Acton company was well-equipped. in his deposition, however, Thomas Thorp, of Captain Davis' company stated that he didn't have a cartridge box until the morning of April 19, when he was given one by Dr. Smith as he passed his house.[64] Thorp may have been the exception to the rule in Davis' company, as we know from the August 14, 1835 deposition of Hannah Leighton (the wife of Captain Davis in 1775) that a "considerable number" of the Acton minute men came to their captain's house to roll cartridges for their cartridge boxes

---

[61] French, General Gage's Informers, "Captain Laurie's Report to General Gage, April 26, 1775," p. 97.

[62] Shattuck, "Declaration of Lt. Edward Thornton Gould," p. 350.

[63] French, The Day of Concord and Lexington, p. 186.

[64] Adams, "Deposition of Thomas Thorp, July 10, 1835," p. 43.

following the alarm on the morning of April 19.[65] It would be nice to know more about the quality of arms carried by Concord and the other companies which marched toward the British on that fateful April day.

In any case, according to the account of Captain Laurie, the colonials marched toward his position on the bridge in "a seeming regular manner."[66] Lt. Sutherland and Ensign Lister also praised the military and orderly manner in which the colonials advanced to the bridge. There was no reason for the march to have been anything but orderly. The Acton Minute Company of Captain Davis, for example, had been drilling twice a week since the preceding November. The town paid them eight pence for each "half day" of drill. The men of the Acton minute men were all volunteers.[67] They were also prideful men, who were conscious of their appearance. According to the 1835 statement of Thomas Thorp, some of the company members were powdering their hair with flour when he arrived on the morning of April 19 at Captain Davis' house.[68]

According to the Acton tradition, which is given some support by Charles Handley's 1835 affidavit, the men of Captain Davis' company marched from Acton to the high ground (muster field) in Concord to the tune of the "White Cockade."[69] Historian George Tolman referred to this tune as "an old Jacobite march intensely galling to the Hanoverians."[70] According to a well-known tradition, repeated by Tolman and French, the column marched to the tune of "The White

---

[65] Ibid., "Affidavit of Hannah Leighton, Aug. 14, 1835," p. 47.

[66] French, General Gage's Informers, "Captain Laurie's Report to General Gage, April 26, 1775," p. 97.

[67] Adams, "Affidavit of Solomon Smith, July 10, 1835," p. 45.

[68] Ibid., "Affidavit of Thomas Thorp, July 10, 1835," p. 43.

[69] Ibid., "Affidavit of Charles Handley, Dec. 1, 1835," p. 47.

[70] Tolman, p. 29.

Cockade" on their way down the hill to the North Bridge. There is little reason to doubt this traditional story, as many companies had fifers and drummers assigned to them. This writer, however, can find no reference to any music played on the march to the bridge in any of the eyewitness accounts of the day. Apparently, the Rev. Ezra Ripley and Lemuel Shattuck either thought it too unimportant to mention or had no evidence of it, as their accounts don't contain any reference to music during the approach to the North Bridge.

The road from Groton ran down the hill past Captain David Brown's house and then wound to the left near the bottom of the hill where it was joined by the road to Colonel Barrett's farm. On its final approach to the North Bridge, the road ran over a straight causeway. At this point it was bordered on the right by the Concord River and on the left by a low lying marsh, which was often flooded in the springtime by the rising waters of the Concord. As the colonials marched down this road, Captain Laurie ordered his men to withdraw to the east side of the bridge and form for "street firing."[71]

The street firing formation was designed to defend a narrow passage such as a street or bridge. For example, the men were formed by platoons into a column. Upon order from the commanding officer, the officer in charge of the first platoon would order his men to fire. The front rank would fire from a kneeling position, while the second and third ranks would fire from a standing position. The second and third ranks would be in the "lock" arms position when firing (i.e., the third rank would project the muzzles of their muskets forward of the men standing in the second rank). After discharging their muskets, the men would come immediately to the "recover" position and, upon order, turn to the left and right (depending on their position) and march down the sides of the column, where they would reunite in the rear and reload.[72]

[71] Lister, p. 27.

[72] French, The Day of Concord and Lexington, p. 195.

This formation was so designed that it could be used to defend a fixed position or in advancing or retreating situations. To maintain a stationary position, the second platoon would move forward as soon as the first had vacated its position, and fire from the same location. To advance, the second platoon went beyond the place where the first platoon had fired; to withdraw, it fired from its own position as soon as the first platoon was out of the way. The rear platoons would adjust their positions according to the direction and pace of the leaders.[73]

In the implementation of this formation, Captain Laurie ordered his own company, the 43rd, to flank the 4th and 10th regiment companies, who were lined up in the road just east of the bridge in the street firing formation.[74] It should be noted that the British position was flanked on the left and right by open fields, which ran down a gentle decline to the river. From this position on the flanks, Laurie hoped that the men of his 43rd could better hit the forward flanks of the American column with a slanting fire. In the meantime, Laurie expected that his men in the street firing formation could pour a deadly raking fire down the ranks of the advancing Provincial column.

Captain Laurie's choice of the street firing formation was probably a good one. In theory, the rotating front ranks could direct repeated volleys of musket fire at the colonials with little time between volleys. In addition, by deploying his 43rd to the flanks, Laurie had increased his potential for firepower. The flankers would also provide valuable flank protection should Laurie decide to conduct an orderly withdrawal from his position just east of the bridge.

About the same time the colonials had started their march down the hill, Lt. Robinson returned from Concord Center accompanied by Captain Lumm, who told Laurie that Smith would send immediate reinforcements. Seeing that the

---

[73] Ibid., p. 195.

[74] French, General Gage's Informers, "Captain Laurie's Report to General Gage, April 26, 1775," p. 97.

Americans had begun their advance, Captain Lumm galloped off to hasten the arrival of the reinforcements. To give him more time to form his street firing formation, Captain Laurie had approved a suggestion from other officers to raise the planks on the bridge. Lt. Sutherland, being the last over the bridge, raised the first plank.[75] Even though he was outnumbered at least four to one, Laurie hoped that he could delay the colonials for the short time it would take for the reinforcements to arrive.

As noted earlier, the Provincials approached the bridge in a column of double files, a formation normally used to move troops along a narrow route. It is mainly a routine marching formation and not an assault formation. The main weakness of a column formation is that it doesn't provide much firepower to the front or rear. The road was narrow, but still wide enough to accommodate more than the two files of soldiers the colonial leaders sent down it. Why didn't they try to increase their firepower to the front? It must be remembered that Colonel Barrett had no desire to provoke the British. Perhaps he thought the bridge guard would withdraw or open their ranks and let him pass.

As Major Buttrick approached the bridge along the straight causeway, he ordered Lt. Sutherland and several soldier assistants to cease the removal of planks from the bridge. Sutherland and the few men helping him went to the east side of the bridge where he jumped over the wall bordering Rev. William Emerson's cow pasture in compliance with Laurie's plan to line the opposite side of the river on each side of the bridge with flankers. Lt. Sutherland tried to get more flankers into the field but only succeeded in getting three or four men over the wall.[76] Sutherland and the few men that followed him into the Old Manse field were quite exposed to the musketry from the men on the American right flank, as the cover in 1775 was not anywhere as dense as it is now.

---

[75] Ibid., "Lt. Sutherland's Letter to General Gage's Secretary, April 27, 1775," pp. 89-90.

[76] Ibid., p. 90.

There is little doubt that the execution of Laurie's plan to flank the 4th and 10th regiment companies with flankers from his 43rd was a miserable failure. For example, Plate III of the Doolittle Prints shows only three men in the left flank position (Old Manse Field). Lt. John Barker, an eye witness and participant in the North Bridge fight offered the following criticism of Captain Laurie:

"Capt. L_____e made his men retire to this side the bridge, which by the bye he ought to have done at first and then he wou'd have had disposition, but at this time he had not, for the Rebels were got so near him that his people were obliged to form the best way they cou'd as soon as they were over the bridge, the three companies got one behind the other so that only the front one could fire."[77]

Barker's above statement, when carefully considered, leaves doubt as to Lt. Barker's understanding of the purpose of Laurie's street firing formation. If a lieutenant failed to comprehend Laurie's intent, many of the enlisted soldiers must have also misinterpreted his intentions. Perhaps they heard the order, but had not been drilled in it recently. As a mixed unit, they were not used to the officers assigned to them. These factors, when combined with the short time they had to prepare their formation once they were ordered to the east side of the bridge, may account for their confusion and failure to properly implement Captain Laurie's order. On the other hand, Laurie had tasked a company from his own 43rd regiment to execute the flanking function. Surely they were used to taking orders from him. Laurie, however, was acting as commander of the whole force at the bridge. He probably left the command of his company to a lieutenant. It is quite probable that he was nearer the bridge where his order to fire could be heard by Lt. Gould of the 4th regiment. Still one somehow expects professional soldiers to do a better job in executing a relatively simple formation.

---

[77] Dana, "Lt. Barker's Diary Account," p. 34.

As Major Buttrick drew near to the bridge, he could see that the three planks the British had removed would not be enough to retard his passage. Across the bridge he could see the British soldiers forming into what Buttrick must have regarded as a threatening formation. He was, however, bound by perhaps the most difficult orders a soldier can receive. He could not fire until his men were fired on first by the British. Colonel Barrett had repeatedly stressed this condition a number of times that morning. In fact, it was one of the cardinal points of policy adhered to by the colonial leaders in Massachusetts. Under no condition did the colonials wish to appear to be the aggressors.

Historians have never satisfactorily determined who fired first on Lexington Common. It appears, however, that the British fired first at the North Bridge. According to Corporal Amos Barrett of Captain David Brown's minute company:

"Capt. Davis had got I be leave within 15 rods of the B when they fire 3 guns one after the other, I see the balls strike in the river on the right of me, as soon as they fird them they fird on us, their balls whisled well..."[78]

Lt. Barker also conceded that the British fired first. In Barker's own words:

"...the rebels when they got near the bridge halted and fronted filling the road from the top to the bottom. The fire soon began from a dropping shot on our side, when they and the front Comny. fired almost at the same instant..."[79]

Although Lt. Sutherland believed the Americans fired first, Captain Laurie believed that a man of his own 43rd company, who was afterwards killed, fired the first shot.[80] As the 43rd had

---

[78] French, The Concord Fight, "An Account by Amos Barrett," p. 13.

[79] Dana, "Lt. John Barker's Diary, April 19, 1775," p. 34.

[80] French, General Gage's Informers, "Captain Laurie's Report to General Gage, April 26, 1775," p. 97.

been ordered to flank the 4th and 10th, it is possible that the man who fired first did so from a flank position in the Old Manse field. This would be consistent with the American reports of balls striking the river to their right.

The first British shots have been interpreted by some historians as warning shots. Captain Laurie, however, omits any mention of ordering warning shots fired. Lt. Barker refers to them only as "dropping shot." In any event, the first three shots, perhaps fired in warning, were quickly followed by more damaging fire from the British side. According to Acton Minute Man Thomas Thorp's affidavit: "I saw a ball strike the water on my right, and some other guns were fired over our heads. A volley was then discarged at us, and Luther Blanchard, our fifer, was wounded."[81]

According to historian Lemuel Shattuck, the ball that wounded Blanchard of Acton also wounded Jonas Brown of Captain David Brown's minute man company. In any event, the British had spilled American blood, and Major Buttrick was now free to return the fire. According to Solomon Smith of Captain Davis's company, Major Buttrick, upon hearing Blanchard cry out, ordered his men to "Fire, for God's sake fire."[82]

Buttrick's urgent order to fire was repeated many times down through the length of the American column. In response, all that could fire without hitting their own men did so. In the British fire that followed, Captain Isaac Davis took a ball in the chest that ended his life. Nineteen-year-old Private Abner Hosmer, a fifer in the Acton company, was also instantly killed by a ball that struck him under the left eye. Amos Barrett thought it strange that more Americans were not killed, but he said the British "fired to high."[83]

---

[81] Adams, "Thomas Thorp's Affidavit, July 10, 1835," p. 43.

[82] Ibid., "Solomon Smith's Affidavit, July 10, 1835," p. 45.

[83] French, The Concord Fight, "An Account by Amos Barrett," p. 13.

In order to get off a clear shot at the "Redcoats," many of the Americans doubtless broke to the sides of the road, some standing, others firing from kneeling positions. Every man tried to get in a shot, even those beyond effective musket range. Some rushed forward to form a front with the Acton company, others probably fired from where they stood in the column by elevating their muskets to fire over the heads of their fellow patriots. As Allen French pointed out, the Doolittle print shows the whole American column, not only near the bridge but to the rear on the rising road, belching musket smoke.

On the British side of the bridge, confusion prevailed. Only a few soldiers followed Lt. Sutherland into the Old Manse field and two of those were cut down by the Provincial fire. Lt. Sutherland, had reloaded and was in the act of firing again when he was struck above the right breast by a musket ball.[84] Perhaps the wounding of Lt. Gould and Kelly was even a greater blow to the British as these two officers were in charge of the two companies that had been drawn up in the street firing formation. The failure of these companies to properly execute Laurie's street firing formation was a key factor in the British failure to hold the bridge. Lt. Edward Hull of Laurie's 43rd was also wounded in the right breast in the North Bridge skirmish (Hull would later receive two more wounds on the road back, dying on May 2, 1775 in Menotomy). With Laurie occupied with the command of the whole and Lt. Hull wounded, the chances of the 43rd executing an effective flanking action were diminished. The high casualty rate among the officers within a minute or so of the firing did not help the British cause.

The skirmish at the North Bridge did not last but a minute or two. Outgunned, their street firing formation a failure, the British soldiers broke ranks and ran. Captain Laurie briefly described the situation to General Gage as follows:

"A general popping from them ensued, the Company of the 4th Regiment gave afire, as did a few of my own from the flanks, after which the

---

[84] Lister, pp. 27-28.

whole went to the right about, in spite of all that could be done to prevent them."[85]

As the British conducted their hasty retreat, the minute men poured onto the bridge in pursuit of their fleeing foe. in his quaint words, Amos Barrett has left us with an account of the disorderly retreat:

"When I got over their was 2 lay ded and a nother allmost ded, we did not foiler them. Their was 8 or 10 that was wounded and a running and hobbling about lucking back to see if we was after them."[86]

The picture Corporal Barrett has left us of the British withdrawal is that of a pathetic rout. How quickly adverse circumstances can change proud soldiers into men whose main thoughts turn to self-survival. Was their failure to hold the bridge longer caused by the overwhelming odds they faced, or by poor leadership combined with lack of combat experience and recent street firing drill? We can only speculate. Perhaps it was a combination of all those reasons. In any event, history recorded the first effective armed colonial resistance to British military power on April 19 as occurring at Concord's North Bridge. Here also occurred the first British combat deaths in the Revolutionary War. As the British conducted their hasty retreat from the North Bridge, they left one man dead and another seriously wounded. Another dying man was carried off by his fleeing comrades. This was Private James Marr of the 4th regiment, which, due to its position at the head of the bridge, was hit the hardest by the American musketry. Marr, a native of Aberdeen, Scotland, had served in Pitcairn's advance guard on the march out.[87] When the

---

[85] French, <u>General Gage's Informers</u>, "Captain Laurie's Report to General Gage, April 26, 17-75," p. 97.

[86] French, <u>The Concord Fight</u>, "An Account by Amos Barrett," p. 13.

[87] French, <u>The Day of Concord and Lexington</u>, p. 105 (footnote)

British withdrew from Concord, Marr was left in the care of Concord citizens. Marr was listed in the April 24, 1775 muster roll of the 4th regiment as "died." As late as April 23, however, he was well enough to sign a deposition to indicate that the British fired first at the North Bridge.[88] In regard to his casualties at the North Bridge, Laurie's April 26 report to General Gage would state: "At the Bridge 4 officers were wounded, 3 Privates killed. A Serg. and four wounded. The Enemy's loss uncertain."[89]

The four officers to receive wounds represented one half of the officers present in the three companies defending the bridge.

As the fleeing British reached the top of the road leading to the bridge, the road turned to the right and continued to Concord Center past the Rev. William Emerson's house on the right and Elisha Jones's house on the left. Some of the Regulars may have taken a short cut through Rev. Emerson's field. There is a story, based on a Jones family tradition, that Elisha Jones, a blacksmith and a member of one of Concord's militia companies, grabbed a musket and pointed it out the northwest second floor bedroom window at the retreating British soldiers. According to this tradition, Jones' wife Elizabeth, realizing that if he fired, Jones would place the family in great danger, wrestled the musket from his grasp. Jones, it is said, went downstairs unarmed and stood in his doorway looking at the passing redcoats. One British soldier, according to the tradition, resented something about Jones' appearance, perhaps a look of scorn or triumph, and fired a hasty shot at the unarmed man. The musket ball missed its mark by about a yard and pierced the shed near the doorway. To this day, the Elisha Jones House is better known locally as the "Bullet Hole House," although historians doubt if the present bullet hole was made by a musket ball of 1775 vintage.[90]

---

[88] Shattuck, "Deposition of James Marr, April 23, 1775," p. 349.

[89] French, General Gage's Informers, "Captain Laurie's Report to General Gage, April 26, 1775," p. 97.

[90] John F. Luzader, Historic Structures Report, Historical Data Section, Part II, National Park Service, 1968, pp. 14-16.

This tradition is based on a story told to Judge John Shepard Keyes, a nineteenth century owner of the house, by Elisha's daughter Mary sometime before her death in 1853. Mary was only four years old in April of 1775, and the story was published by Judge Keyes about a decade after Mary's death in his Story of an old House. Unfortunately, no other evidence has surfaced to confirm the Jones family tradition relating to the controversial bullet hole.[91]

The reader might wonder why Jones was not with his militia company. According to the family tradition, he chose to remain at home to guard his hearth and family. Shattuck states, however, that Jones's house was used as storage for barrels of beef and about 17,000 pounds of salt fish belonging to the Province's military stores.[92] Perhaps Elisha Jones stayed at home also to better safeguard the military stores, if any remained in his shed and cellar at the time of the bridge fight.

The colonials did not pursue the retreating British towards the town center. Instead of following the road to the right, the leading companies went up the hill and took up positions behind a stone wall which ran along the ridge east of the road. Not all the minute and militia men went to this new position east of the bridge. According to the account of Thaddeus Blood of Captain Nathan Barrett's company, "part of our men went over the bridge and myself among the rest and part returned to the ground that had left."[93]

The reader may wonder why the provincial force did not immediately continue their advance on the town as they had earlier intended. After all, they were highly successful in rushing the bridge and their casualties were few; in addition to the deaths of Davis and Hosmer, and the wounding of Blanchard and Brown, the following two men were slightly wounded: Captain

---

[91] Ibid., p. 15.

[92] Shattuck, p. 98.

[93] Blood, p. 2.

Davis's brother Ezekiel, and Joshua Brooks of Lincoln. The two latter individuals received grazing wounds to the head area.[94] Ezekiel Davis was a member of his brother Isaac's minute man company while Brooks was a member of Smith's minute company. In his letter, Amos Barrett states that after he got over the bridge, he saw the British marching up the road from Concord. In his own words Barrett stated:

"We then saw the hull body acoming out of town we then was orded to lay bahind a wall that run over a hill, and when they got my anuff Mager Buttrick said he wood give the word fire but they did not come quite so near as he expected before tha halted."[95]

The British Corporal Barrett saw were, of course, the reinforcements Captain Laurie had requested. For some reason, Lt. Col. Francis Smith placed himself at the head of the detachment of reinforcements from town. According to Ensign Lister, the reinforcements consisted of the 47th Grenadiers. On the other hand, Lt. Barker said Smith led two or three companies to the bridge. In any event, for reasons best known to him, Lt. Col. Smith led the reinforcements. Lt. Barker described the scene as follows:

"the Coll. order'd 2 or 3 Compys. but put himself at their head by which means stopt 'em from being time enough, for being a very fat heavey man he wou'd not have reached the bridge in half an hour tho' it was not half a mile to it..."[96]

Perhaps Smith chose to lead the reinforcements because after the carnage and disorder that occurred on Lexington Common,

---

[94] Ellen Chase, The Beginnings of the American Revolution, Vol. III, Sir Isaac Pitman and Sons, Ltd. London, 1911, p. 37.

[95] French, The Concord Fight, "An Account by Amos Barrett," pp. 13-14.

[96] Dana, "Lt. John Barker's Diary, April 19, 1775," p. 34.

he didn't want to entrust a detached command to any of the officers he had with him at Concord. Although he arrived too late to help Laurie at the bridge, the sight of his approaching grenadiers checked the American advance. His grenadiers then provided cover for the retreating British until they had an opportunity to reform their disorganized ranks. The company of the 4th regiment, however, had been hit hard at the bridge, and according to Ensign Lister, it was doubtful if the 4th ever got together again that day as an organized unit.[97]

The grenadiers in Smith's reinforcement force probably got no further on the road to the bridge than the vicinity of Elisha Jones' house. According to the affidavit of the Acton Minute Man Solomon Smith:

"I do not know what proportion of the Americans followed over the bridge; but our company, and the Concord minute-men, and very many others, proceeded to an eminence, on the east side of the road, back of Elisha Jone's house, behind a wall. It was, perhaps, forty rods from where the enemy had halted. After a short time we dispersed, and without any regularity, went back over the bridge."[98]

It is interesting to note the four little lines someone drew on the before-mentioned MacKenzie Map. As Allen French pointed out, these lines may represent the furthermost advance of Smith's relief force. The map wasn't drawn to scale, but it would appear to this writer that the four marks are about opposite where the Elisha Jones house would be if it was drawn in on the so-called MacKenzie Map.

In any case, Major Buttrick apparently chose not to attack the British with his force on the hill unless they attempted to dislodge his men from their position. Lt. Col. Smith was, of course, under limited orders to destroy military supplies. He had no mandate to kill New Englanders unless they attacked him

---

[97] Lister, p. 28.

[98] Adams, "Affidavit of Solomon Smith, July 10, 1835," p. 45.

first. Moreover, the Yankees were ensconced in a strong defensive position with reinforcements not far away, where they had withdrawn to the high ground west of the bridge that they had earlier vacated. Obviously, an assault on the Provincials nearest his position would not only be dangerous, but might prove hard to explain later on to General Gage.

Apparently, Lt. Col. Smith conducted a conference with his officers as Amos Barrett reports:

"The Commanding offersr ordred the hull Battalion to halt and offersrs to the frunt march, the offersrs then marched to the front thair we lay behind the wall about 200 of us with our guns cockd exspecting every minit to have the word fire. Our orders was if we fird to fire 2 or 3 times and then retreat. If we fird I beleave we could kild all most every officseer thair was in the front, but we had no orders to fire and their want a gun fird. They staid about 10 minits and then marched back and we after them."[99]

It is obvious that Major Buttrick had reverted to the conservative policy that the colonials had maintained all morning in that he would not fire on the British unless fired upon first. The British at 40 rods, moreover, were beyond effective musket range. In the days of the one-shot flintlock musket, an average soldier had a reasonably good chance of hitting a man-sized figure between 50 to 80 yards. After 80 yards distance, the odds of hitting a man gradually decreased until at 200 yards only an extremely lucky shot would find the target actually aimed at. Smith was well aware of the effective musket range of the flintlocks of the day, and it is hard to believe he would endanger his force by keeping them within the effective range of Major Buttrick's men.

According to Amos Barrett, Smith lingered only a short time in the road and then marched back to Concord Center. Barrett says that "They staid about 10 minutes and then marched back and we after them." The weight of existing documentation and tradition indicates that the minute and militia men withdrew back

---

[99] French, The Concord Fight, "An Account by Amos Barrett," p. 14.

across the river and resumed their former position on the high ground overlooking the North Bridge. According to the accepted interpretation, some of the men who were present at the bridge fight cut across the Great Meadows to wait for the British at Meriam's Corner. After the brief exchange of fire at Meriam's Corner, many of the men followed the British back towards Boston. Perhaps this is what Barrett meant in regard to following the British back. The reader should remember that Barrett wrote his report many years after the fact.

The careful reader by now should be aware that Colonel James Barrett's force deviated from the original intent to go to the aid of Concord, which earlier they thought the British were burning. According to the tradition repeated by Shattuck, the Provincial military leaders "resolved to march into the middle of the town to defend their homes, or die in the attempt."[100] For some reason never explained, they abandoned their earlier purpose and resumed the waiting and watching game on the high ground west of the river. Historians can only speculate as to the reasons they did not stick to the original plan. Perhaps the smoke had died down and they realized the British were not going to burn the town down. Perhaps also, Colonel Barrett realized that it was too late to save the military supplies and an attack on the British would only provoke them into torching the town. Moreover, Colonel Barrett, after the North Bridge fight, may have come to the realization that his force was inadequate to dislodge the British from Concord until additional reinforcements arrived.

There is another facet concerning the North Bridge fight that has never been explained to the satisfaction of historians and a few later day military professionals. Why didn't Colonel Barrett and his entire militia force follow Major Buttrick and the leading companies over the bridge? Instead of following Buttrick, the reader will recall that many of the militia withdrew to the high ground "Muster Field" they had recently departed. It should be noted also that they carried the bodies of Captain Davis and

---

[100] Shattuck, p. 111.

Abner Hosmer with them. According to Amos Baker, the bodies of the two slain minute men were laid out in one of the rooms of Major John Buttrick's nearby house.

The question is, why did Colonel Barrett split his force into two groups, thus weakening it? The extant documentation is silent on this matter. One popular theory is that the militia colonel lost control of his command due to the general disorganization that seemed to prevail following the brief North Bridge encounter. Of this disorganization there is ample documentation; for example, Concord's Thaddeus Blood stated "After the fire (North Bridge fight) every one appeared to be his own commander."[101] Acton's Thomas Thorp is even more specific concerning the disorder following the North Bridge fight.

"Our company, and most of the others, pursued, but in great disorder, and went to an eminence back of Elisha Jones, and stood behind a wall, forty rods, or more, from where the British had joined a reinforcement. In a short time we returned over the bridge, but did not form in any order. As we stood there, the detachment from Col. Barrett's returned, and passed us, and might easily have been taken prisoners, if we had not been in such confusion. I do not remember that any one was there, who assumed any command."[102]

The reader should note that the above testimony was taken many years after the fact during the peak of the controversy between Acton historian Josiah Adams and Concord historian Lemuel Shattuck. Thorpe's recollections of 60 years past were doubtless encouraged by the relentless Adams, who was highly critical of the Concord military leaders on April 19, 1775. Nevertheless, the theme of confusion among the American ranks following the North Bridge fight is both supported in tradition and the documents that have come down to us.

---

[101] Blood, p. 2.

[102] Adams, "Affidavit of Thomas Thorp, July 10, 1835," p. 44.

In this writer's opinion, Barrett, who was positioned toward the rear, seeing the confusion that prevailed after the bridge skirmish, and noting Smith's relief force coming up the road, used his influence to check the advance of the rear companies and led them back up the hill. He probably believed the whole British force was with Smith, and that his force was not large enough or sufficiently organized to take on the professional soldiers Smith had with him.

It would appear, perhaps, that Colonel Barrett lost a good opportunity to inflict a really serious blow to Smith's regulars when part of his column withdrew to the west of the bridge. Had his column stayed together in a disciplined force, they should have been able to defeat the combined force of Laurie and Smith's relief column. However, once Smith withdrew with Laurie's men to Concord, Barrett's decision not to attack the British in town was probably a wise one. Laurie's losses at the North Bridge did not significantly weaken Smith's force. After all, he still had about 500 professional soldiers under his command at Concord Center and more on the way from the South Bridge. Captain Parsons was also due to return shortly, although his force was in danger of being cut off. To attack and successfully dislodge a force as large as Smith's, even under ideal conditions of command and control, which were not present, Colonel Barrett would have required a much larger force then he had.

It should be noted that there is much we don't know about the events that occurred between about 10 a.m. and noon, when Lt. Col. Frances Smith started back to Boston. According to the Rev. Ezra Ripley, many of the Americans took advantage of the lull in the action following the North Bridge fight and ate breakfast.[103] The Rev. Thaxter, for one, visited his fellow cleric, the Rev. William Emerson for rest and refreshment. One can easily imagine the Rev. Thaxter, pistols bulging in his pockets, ardently expressing his views with the equally patriotic Whig minister from Concord. It has been often said that the

---

[103] Ripley, pp. 29-30.

Congregational clergy were among the leading opponents of Crown government in the Province of Massachusetts Bay. Certainly, they were deeply and personally involved in the struggle for social justice as they saw it.

History records one sad incident in the interval between the North Bridge fight and the return of Captain Parsons' relief force from Colonel Barrett's farm. A British soldier of the 4th regiment, apparently seriously wounded, was left near the North Bridge by his fleeing comrades. While in this pitiful condition, according to historian Ruth Wheeler, Ammi White, a twenty or twenty-one year old minute man in Captain David Brown's company came along and noticed the fallen soldier.[104] Apparently, for reasons best known to White, the young man dispatched the unfortunate Briton with a stroke or two from his hatchet or tomahawk. Later, when Captain Parsons and his four companies returned from Barrett's farm, the soldiers, upon seeing the mutilated head of the luckless victim, mistook the ghastly wound for an intentional scalping. Later, when they reached town, Parsons' men spread the rumor that the Yankees were scalping those who fell into their clutches. In fact, Ensign Jeremy Lister exaggerated the sad incident even further. According to Lister:

"At this place (North Bridge) there was 4 men of the 4th Company killed who afterwards scalp'd their eyes goug'd their noses and ears cut off, such barbarity exercis'd upon the Corps could scarcely be paralelld by the most uncivilised savages...[105]

Later, the Provincial Congress, in order to refute this story which enjoyed wide circulation in the Boston press, ordered depositions taken from the two Americans who dug the graves of the two British soldiers killed at the bridge. According to the

---

[104] Ruth R. Wheeler, Concord Climate for Freedom, Concord Antiquarian Society, Concord, 1967, p. 228.

[105] Lister, p. 27.

deposition of Zechariah Brown and Thomas Davis, Jr., neither of the two soldiers they buried were scalped or missing ears.[106]

Earlier Concord historians ignored the unfortunate incident in their narratives, but, according to the Concord historian Ruth Wheeler, the name of the hatchet swinging minute man was passed on privately from historian to historian. This name was Ammi White, who this writer has seen listed in the Concord Town records as having been paid for his services on April 19th as a minute man. Nathaniel Hawthorne, in his day, speculated that the perpetrator of the act was a loutish boy employed by the Rev. William Emerson in chopping wood behind the Old Manse. According to Hawthorne's version, the boy suffered pangs of remorse for the rest of his life.[107] The Rev. Emerson's granddaughter in her letter of 1888 stated that the only person that could possibly be chopping wood at the Old Manse on such a day as April 19 would be the family slave, and she denied that the family slave was the hatchet wielding culprit.[108]

The historical evidence pointing to Ammi White as the perpetrator of the brutal "coup de grace" at the North Bridge is far from conclusive, and is of only side interest to us today. It is important to the narration of the events of April 19, 1775, however, because of the effect of the scalping rumor had on the British soldiers. It doubtless hardened their minds against the individual Massachusetts militiaman, and may also have contributed to the looting and murder of several unarmed Massachusetts citizens along the road back to Boston.

As mentioned earlier, Captain Lawrence Parsons of the 10th Regiment of Foot had led a detachment to Colonel Barrett's farm to search for cannon and any other military supplies that may have been concealed there. Fortunately, Colonel Barrett had been alerted in advance, and was able to make provisions for the

---

[106] Shattuck, p. 350.

[107] Wheeler, p. 228.

[108] French, The Day of Concord and Lexington, p. 214.

concealment of the cannon. According to an old Concord tradition, he had his men dismantle the cannon barrels from their carriages and carried the barrels into his corn field, where a thin covering of dirt was placed over them. In the garret of the house, Mrs. Barrett had concealed casks of musket balls, cutlasses, and flint by placing feathers over them.[109] While the search of the house was being conducted, the officers asked Mrs. Barrett to provide them with food and drink. One of the sergeants wanted strong spirits, but Captain Parsons prevented the sergeant from drinking as he might become unfit for duty. According to the tradition, Mrs. Barrett at first refused payment for the food as she felt it was her Christian duty to feed her enemies. According to Shattuck, however, the officers forced money on her and she reluctantly accepted with the remark "This is the price of blood."[110] The officers almost arrested Colonel Barrett's son Stephen mistaking him for Colonel Barrett. Mrs. Barrett convinced them, however, that Stephen was not the "master of the house" and they didn't arrest the young man. According to Shattuck, however, the British stole some money from one of the rooms.

The British didn't find the cannons or the military supplies stored in the attic. They did, however, find some gun carriages, which, according to the Rev. Ripley, they burned in the road. On the other hand, Shattuck claimed that before the British could burn the gun carriages, shots were heard from the North Bridge and they withdrew.[111]

Shattuck's contention that Parsons' detachment heard the round of the musketry at the North Bridge is not supported by the affidavit of Charles Handley of Acton. At the time of the North Bridge fight, Handley, a thirteen-year-old boy, lived at the tavern kept by Mrs. Brown. This tavern was located about half

---

[109] Ripley, p. 21.

[110] Shattuck, p. 109.

[111] Ibid.

way between the North Bridge and Colonel Barrett's farm. According to Handley, the British upon their return from Barrett's, halted at the tavern, where three of four officers went inside to partake in some spirits. The soldiers of the detachment remained outside by the roadside and, according to Handley, some drink was carried outside to them. While the British were resting by the roadside, Handley heard shots from the North Bridge, but he claimed that the British soldiers didn't appear to hear them. According to Handley, the British marched away from Brown's Tavern shortly thereafter, but they were not in any haste.[112]

Handley's affidavit, even though it was made in 1835, has a ring of truth about it. The experiences of youth are often retained in the memory in more vivid form than experiences gained in later years. Moreover, it is logical that Parsons should not bypass the opportunity the tavern offered to refresh his troops after their hard morning's work. Shattuck's remark that the British failed to burn the gun carriages at Barrett's farm because they were interrupted by the musketry at the North Bridge is neither supported by Rev. Ripley's account, written earlier, or Handley's affidavit. Ensign DeBerniere's report to General Gage also mentions that the British destroyed some military stores at Colonel Barrett's.[113]

Following their stop for refreshment at the Widow Brown's Tavern, the four companies under Captain Parsons continued their march to rejoin the main body in Concord Center. As they approached the area of the North Bridge they were discomforted by the sight of Colonel Barrett's men on the high ground west of the bridge. The fact that there was no sign of the three companies left in the vicinity of the bridge must also have distressed them. Colonel Barrett did not attack them, however, and they were allowed to cross the North Bridge unscathed. The recollection of the Acton Minute Man Solomon Smith is very

---

[112] Adams, "Affidavit of Charles Handley, Dec. 1, 1835," pp. 46-47.

[113] Kehoe, The British Soldiers, "Ensign DeBerniere's Report to General Gage," p. 121.

similar to that of his comrade in arms Thomas Thorp. According to Smith:

"While we were there (Muster Field), the detachment which had been to destroy stores at Col. Barrett's, returnd, and passed us without molestation. It was owing to our want of order, and our confused state, that they were not taken prisoners."[114]

As Parsons' detachment passed over the North Bridge, they were disturbed by the sight of the two dead soldiers, especially by the terrible head wound of the man who had been slain with the hatchet. Captain Parsons doubtless insured that they were dead, but he didn't take their bodies with him. Probably he feared he was in danger of being attacked and he couldn't spare the soldiers necessary to carry two bodies at the quick pace he wished to march. When carrying bodies, soldiers cannot use their muskets, and Parsons had no way of knowing what ambushes the colonials had prepared for him between the bridge and Concord Center. In any event, dead soldiers could provide no future service to the King and the safety of his command was paramount in Captain Parsons' mind. As events proved, his detachment rejoined Smith in Concord without further incident.

Colonel Barrett has sometimes been criticized for not attacking Parsons' detachment and inflicting a truly damaging blow on the British. It must be remembered, however, that the British still controlled Concord. Perhaps Barrett thought an attack on Parsons would provoke the British into burning the town. Moreover, an attack on Parsons could not save the military stores in Concord from destruction and would, most importantly, be considered an aggressive act by those who would later review the day's events. It should be noted that the unity of command that Colonel Barrett had enjoyed just prior to the bridge fight no longer existed. According to Shattuck, about 150 colonials went immediately across the Great Fields to Meriam's

---

[114] Adams, "Affidavit of Solomon Smith, July 10, 1835," p. 45.

Corner following the North Bridge fight.[115] Unfortunately, Shattuck does not provide documentation for this statement and there is doubt that they went immediately to Meriam's Corner. In any event, Barrett's force was reduced by the men who filtered off to eat breakfast or to check on the welfare of their families. It is quite possible that Colonel Barrett's organizational problems influenced him not to attack Parsons' 128 or so men. In any case, it seems apparent that Colonel Barrett at this point had reverted back to his earlier policy of not firing on the British unless they attacked him first.

It was probably about 10 a.m. or shortly thereafter, that Captain Parsons re-crossed the North Bridge. Here it should be noted that our historical knowledge of the events that occurred in the remaining two hours of the British occupation of Concord is incomplete. We do know, however, that Captain Mundy Pole rejoined Smith with the detachment he had taken to the South Bridge. Pole's detachment had searched several houses in the South Bridge area with no apparent success. Some of the British, however, succeeded in obtaining breakfast from area residents. According to Shattuck, Pole kept his men at the South Bridge until they heard the firing from the North Bridge fighting. Before leaving the bridge, Pole's men rendered it impassable by pulling up the planks.[116] We also know that Lt. Col. Smith was concerned for the welfare of his wounded men. Men too seriously wounded for travel were lodged in the nearby homes of Concord residents. Transportation was also arranged for the wounded who couldn't march. For example, a chaise was commandeered from Reuben Brown and another one from John Beaton.[117]

For the officer in the field, the local taverns he encounters are often utilized, not only as places of rest and refreshment, but as

---

[115] Shattuck, p. 112.

[116] Ibid., p. 109.

[117] Ibid., pp. 113-114.

temporary field headquarters. In Wright's Tavern an interesting tradition has developed concerning Major Pitcairn. According to this tradition, which Shattuck repeated, Pitcairn ordered a glass of brandy and stirred it with his bloody finger, while commenting that "He hoped he should stir the damned Yankee blood so before night."[118] Some modern historians have expressed doubt that the fifty-three year old Pitcairn would have made such a boast, as it was not compatible with his image gained from other sources. Nevertheless, it was believed at the time and helped to stamp Pitcairn's unfavorable image in the minds of the American reading public for years to come. This writer can find nothing to either support or refute this old Concord tradition.

Historians have criticized Smith for the time he remained in Concord after Captain Parsons and Pole rejoined his main force with their detachments. Certainly, the clock was not in his favor, as the more time that elapsed the more the odds against him increased. If Smith had known of the large force that was gathering against him, he would doubtless have left Concord earlier. For example, the Town of Danvers in Essex County, some 27 miles from Concord, had been told of the fighting on Lexington Common some time after 8 a.m. Upon receiving this news, Captain Samuel Eppes galloped to Salem where he alerted his Regimental Commander, Colonel Timothy Pickering. Colonel Pickering gave Captain Eppes verbal orders to march, and the Danvers Captain sped back to Danvers, where he had his men on the road before 10 a.m. Not long afterwards, the colonel followed with a large body of his Essex regiment estimated at 300 men.[119] Of course, these companies had little chance of reaching Concord before the British left, but they hoped to cut the British off somewhere on Smith's route back to Boston. In the meantime, Lt. Col. Smith lingered with his troops in Concord. Doubtless he was waiting for the reinforcements he

---

[118] Ibid., p. 113.

[119] James Duncan Phillips, Salem in the Eighteenth Century, Essex Institute, Salem, 1969, p. 363.

had sent back for while he was in Menotomy. He had no way of knowing that, due to the mishandling of an order, these reinforcements would be delayed for hours.

At some point after the North Bridge fight, an estimated 150 men, according to Shattuck, cut across the Great Meadows and took up a position near Meriam's Corner, about a mile east of Concord Center. What orders this force was given prior to taking their new position is unclear. They were, of course, the men who had taken part in the North Bridge fight and probably represented several companies and a mix of individuals from the various towns that were present at the bridge. Who was in command of this force is not known today. Many of the people who cut across the Great Meadows probably did so on their own initiative. As they waited for the British withdrawal from Concord, they doubtless discussed their next move. Unknown to them, additional militia and minute units from Billerica, Chelmsford, and Reading would soon join the victors of the bridge at Meriam's Corner.

In Concord Lt. Col. Francis Smith could delay no longer. He would have to chance meeting the reinforcements somewhere on the road back, if indeed, they were coming. In any case, about noontime he ordered his men up on the road into marching formation. Putting the Light Infantry out to guard his flanks he started his long march (about 18 miles) back to Boston. Thus far his luck had held up pretty good. After all, by leaving Captain Parsons to his fate at the North Bridge, Smith could have lost Parsons and his detachment of 128 or so men. The fact that Parsons returned to Concord with his unit unscathed, was due to the failure of the colonials to attack and not to anything Smith had done to help his Captain. Moreover, Smith had accomplished his mission, although he did so with only limited success. Still, Smith knew that he couldn't be blamed if the Yankees removed much of their military stores to other towns before he arrived.

As Smith marched out of Concord, the grenadiers and marines marched on the road as they did on the march out. Smith was also careful to maintain a strong flanking force of

Light Infantry on the ridge to his left, where the Yankees had been earlier when he marched into town. The ridge, of course, was a likely-looking spot to set up an ambush. In addition, Smith put out flankers on the level plain to his right. He hoped that his flankers would keep the colonials beyond effective musket range of the troops marching in the road. In addition. Smith's column included several chaises, which he had commandeered to haul his North Bridge wounded. Unlike his entry into town, which was accompanied with music, Smith's force marched in silence on the way out of Concord.

About a mile out of town, the long ridge to Smith's left ended at the junction of the Bay Road and the old road to Bedford. Whatever temporary relief Smith may have felt at passing beyond this ridge was quickly lost when he saw the large Massachusetts militia force gathered at and approaching the farmhouse to his left near Meriam's Corner. For Smith and the tired troops that made up his command, the worst was yet to come.

4 – MERIAM'S CORNER

At Meriam's Corner on April 19, 1775, there was a little bridge which spanned Elm Brook, a branch of the Millbrook. The British column passed eastward over this bridge about 12:30 p.m. As the flankers descended the ridge, they strode onto the road in order to cross the brook without wading. In the meantime, a large force of minute and militia men were approaching Meriam's Corner from the north. Others were probably already in position behind or near the structures on the Meriam farm, which was within musket range to the north. As the reader will recall, many colonials who had taken part in the North Bridge fighting had cut across the Great Meadows to wait for the British at or near Meriam's Corner.

One of the companies approaching Meriam's Corner was the Reading Minute Man Company under the command of Captain John Brooks, who would later serve as governor of Massachusetts (1816 - 1823). Following behind Brooks' minute company was another company from Reading under the command of Captain John Bacheller. Coburn's muster rolls list Bacheller as captain of a 61-man minute company of Colonel Ebenezer Bridge's regiment. In his 1825 letter to Daniel Shattuck, however, the Rev. Edmund Foster referred to

Bacheller's command on April 19 as "the militia company of Reading."[1]

The Reading companies were followed by companies from Billerica and Chelmsford. Earlier on the march from Concord, at the intersection of the road from Chelmsford, the Reading men had met Colonel Bridge, the regimental commander of minute men. Colonel Bridge had halted the partial regiment he had gathered for a rest before he continued his march to Concord. As he had recently given his Reading men a rest, Captain Brooks requested and was granted permission to march on ahead of Colonel Bridge and his partial regiment. Colonel Bridge cautioned him, however, not to march too far ahead of the regiment, as Brooks was "unacquainted with the posture of affairs."[2]

Captain John Brooks was a young man who was probably far above average. In civil life, he was a doctor actively engaged in building up his practice of medicine. He also took his military duties seriously. Early in his command he had journeyed to Salem to seek the advice of a recognized military tactician, Colonel Timothy Pickering.[3] The Salem colonel was in the process of writing a new manual of drill entitled "Easy Plan of Discipline for a Militia." Brooks must have learned his lessons well, as later in life he would hold the rank of major-general.

In volunteering his company to march ahead of the regiment, Captain Brooks did not act rashly. He knew that Bridge's partial regiment was close behind, and he could always fall back to it if he ran into any difficulty. He was concerned, however, that he would arrive too late to be of any service.

Equally ardent in the common cause were the men from Billerica. Moreover, they had a special score to settle with the

---

[1] Rev. Ezra Ripley, A History of the Fight at Concord, Allen and Atwell, Concord, 1827, p. 32.

[2] William H. Sumner, A History of East Boston; with Biographical Sketches, J. E. Tilton and Company, Boston, 1858, pp. 355-356.

[3] Ibid.

British, who in the preceding month had tarred and feathered a member of that town, Thomas Ditson. The British had claimed that Ditson had tempted a British soldier to desert while he was arranging for the purchase of a Brown Bess musket in Boston. Ditson, marching in Captain Jonathan Stickney's 54-man minute company, would soon have the opportunity to gain revenge. Other forces from Billerica marching toward Meriam's Corner included Captain Edward Farmer's 35-man militia company and a 12-man contingent under Lt. Oliver Crosby.[4] According to tradition, the Billerica men had marched by way of Bedford and had rested under the old oak tree near Fitch's Tavern with the men from Reading.[5] According to the Rev. Ezra Ripley, the Billerica militia was commanded by Colonel William Thompson of Billerica. Ripley further wrote that the Billerica men arrived at Meriam's Corner a few minutes after the Reading men.[6]

Other companies from Colonel David Green's militia regiment included the 61-man Chelmsford militia company under captain Oliver Barron. Sergeant John Ford, a veteran of the French and Indian War, also marched in Barron's company. Ford numbered among the many Americans who had once fought as allies of the British against Britain's old rival, the French. According to the accepted tradition, Parson Bridge wanted to pray with the Chelmsford men before they marched, but sergeant Ford in his haste to reach Concord could not spare the time for prayer.[7] Ford would later distinguish himself in the fighting eastward of Meriam's Corner.

---

[4] Samuel Adams Drake, History of Middlesex County, Estes and Lauriat, Boston, 1880, p. 264.

[5] Ellen Chase, The Beginnings of the American Revolution, Vol. III, Sir Isaac Pitman and Sons, Ltd., London, 1911, p. 60.

[6] Ripley, pp. 30-31.

[7] Chase, p. 63.

According to the Rev. Ripley, a company from East Sudbury came up near Meriam's Corner on the south side of the road.[8] The Sudbury historian Alfred S. Hudson wrote that this company was probably the militia company commanded by Captain Joseph Smith.[9] From East Sudbury Smith's militia company probably marched through Lincoln to reach its position at or eastward of Meriam's corner. A minute company from Sudbury under Captain John Nixon and a Sudbury militia company under Captain Aaron Haynes had arrived near colonel Barrett's farm just before the British had left that location. These companies were too late for the North Bridge fight, but they or individuals from those companies could have cut across the Great Meadows and joined in the fighting at Meriam's Corner. However, this writer has seen no mention of them at this location, and Hudson only mentions Smith's militia company as having been at Meriam's corner in company strength.

There were probably other companies not far from Meriam's Corner from such towns as Dracut, Stow, and Westford, but what role they played in the fighting, if any, is unclear. Perhaps they were too far off to get a good shot at the British. According to John Galvin, Wilmington was also present at Meriam's Corner with Reading and Billerica, but this writer has seen nothing in regard to Wilmington's role at this location.

The Concord historian Lemuel Shattuck wrote some sixty years after the event that about one hundred and fifty provincials had cut across the "Great Field" to intercept the enemy at Meriam's Corner. According to Shattuck, these men went to Meriam's Corner immediately after the North Bridge fight.[10] Perhaps these recent veterans of the North Bridge fight took up a position on the ridge near Meriam's Corner, but they must have

---

[8] Ripley, p. 31.

[9] Alfred S. Hudson, The History of Sudbury Massachusetts, 1638 1889, The Town of Sudbury, 1889, p. 380.

[10] Lemuel Shattuck, History of the Town of Concord, Russell, Odiorne and Company, Boston, 1835, p. 112.

withdrawn at the approach of the flankers Smith had sent onto the ridge. It would seem logical that they would have withdrawn to the shelter offered by the structures standing on the Meriam farm, but they are not mentioned as being in that location in the letter of the Rev. Edmund Foster, or the published account of William H. Sumner based on the latter's conversations with John Brooks.

There is evidence that at least one colonial who cut across the Great Meadows from the North Bridge took up a position other than at Meriam's Corner. According to Thaddeus Blood of Captain Nathan Barrett's Concord militia company, there was little organization among the colonials who had exchanged fire with the British at the bridge following that encounter. Blood described his position near Meriam's Corner as follows:

> *"After the fire every one apeared to be his own commander it was thot best to go to the east part of the town and take them as they cam back each took his own station, for myself I took my stand south of where Den Minot then lived and saw the British come from Concord their right flanks in the meadows, their left on the hill."*[11]

Deacon Minot's farm, of course, was the next farm east of Meriam's Corner. Blood's position was near enough to Meriam's Corner, however, to see the British left flank on the ridge north of the road and the right flank in the meadows. How many other men of the 150 that Shattuck claimed cut across the Great Meadows took up positions other than at Meriam's Corner is unknown. It would seem, however, from the statement of Blood and others that little organization prevailed among the men who had taken part in the North Bridge fight following that skirmish.

In any event, as Captain John Brooks approached Meriam's Corner at the head of his company, he saw the British left flank guard moving eastward on the long ridge which parallels the old Bay Road to the north. At first he mistook the British flankers

---

[11] Thaddeus Blood, "Thaddeus Blood's Account of April 19, 1775," p. 3, Concord Free Public Library, Concord, Massachusetts.

for members of the Charlestown Artillery Company, who apparently had uniforms similar to the British light infantrymen Brooks saw on the ridge. Upon sight of the soldiers on the ridge, Brooks had halted his minute company and watched as the light infantry flankers filed down the ridge to cross the little bridge at Meriam's Corner behind the long column of the main body in the road.[12] The Rev. Edmund Foster of Littleton was an armed volunteer in Captain Brooks' company that morning and from a distance of about 20 rods, he watched with the Reading men the scene he described as follows:

"The British marched down the hill with very slow, but steady step, without music or a word being spoken that could be heard. Silence reigned on both sides. As soon as the British had gained the main road, and passed a small bridge near that corner, they faced about suddenly, and fired a volley of musketry upon us. They overshot; and no one, to my knowledge, was injured by the fire. The fire was immediately returned by the Americans, and two British soldiers fell dead at a little distance from each other, in the road near the brook. The battle now began, and was carried on with little or no military discipline and order, on the part of the Americans, during the remainder of. that day."[13]

According to Rev. Foster, the British high volley from the rear of the British column was the first firing of shots at Meriam's Corner. The Rev. Foster's account of the action at Meriam's Corner always seemed to this writer to be quite clear and believable. There are other eyewitness accounts, however, which conflict with Rev. Foster's version of the exchange of fire at Meriam's Corner. For example, the British Ensign of His Majesty's 10th Regiment of Foot, Jeremy Lister, indicates that the colonials fired first at Meriam's Corner. According to Ensign Lister's account,

---

[12] Sumner, pp. 355-356.

[13] Ripley, pp. 32-33.

"immediately as we desended the hill into the road the Rebels begun a brisk fire but at so great a distance it was without effect, but as they kept marching nearer when the Granadiers found them within shot they returned their fire just about that time I recd a shot through my right elbow joint which efectually disabled that arme."[14]

Lt. Sutherland who, as the reader will recall, was wounded in the "old Manse" field near the North Bridge was riding somewhere in the column in a commandeered chaise on the way back. Sutherland's version of what may have been the Meriam's Corner fight seems to support the statement of Ensign Lister that the colonials fired first at Meriam's Corner. According to Lt. Sutherland in his April 26, 1775 letter to Sir Henry Clinton, "just at the end of the Town next to this a few concealed villians fired on us, of which we killed 2, but they wounded 2 of ours..."[15]

Of the accounts of the two British officers, Lister's provides the most detail and is more believable because as a member of the flanking party, Lister was probably in a better position to see who fired first than Lt. Sutherland from his seat in the enclosed chaise in which he was riding. There is a good possibility that Sutherland's chaise was located in the middle or near the front of the column. In that case, his account may not be of the fighting at Meriam's Corner, but of fighting to the eastward, perhaps on Hardy's Hill. This writer agrees with the former Park Service historian Robert Ronsheim, who believed that Sutherland's account of the initial fighting on the march back referred to Hardy's Hill and not Meriam's Corner.

In addition to Lister's account, there is another account that supports the view that the Americans fired first at Meriam's Corner. In 1858, William H. Sumner's book entitled <u>A History of East Boston</u> appeared in print. Sumner was a friend of Governor John Brooks, who as a young captain commanded the Reading

---

[14] Jeremy Lister, <u>Concord Fight</u>, Harvard University Press, Cambridge, 1931, p. 29.

[15] Vincent J. R. Kehoe, <u>We Were There! The British Soldiers</u>, "Lt. Wm. Sutherland's Letter to Sir Henry Clinton, April 26, 1775," Chelmsford, Massachusetts, p. 143.

minute man company at Meriam's Corner. Once Sumner had accompanied Brooks when his late friend went to review the Massachusetts Militia near Concord. According to Sumner's book, as they passed Meriam's Corner, Brooks pointed out the barn from which his men attacked the British on April 19, 1775. According to Summer's published account, Captain Brooks, after he decided the soldiers he saw at Meriam's corner were British, ordered his men to advance and take up a position near Meriam's Corner "covered by a barn and the walls around it."[16] According to Sumner, Brooks told him that he then ordered his men to fire "directly at the bridge which was twenty or thirty rods off. As the British army was in great haste to make good its retreat, it fired but one volley in return."[17] Sumner went on to add that he thought the Governor had said that nine British soldiers were found "hors de combat" on or near the bridge.

Sumner's recollection of what John Brooks said regarding British casualties at Meriam's Corner would indicate that the British received significant casualties at or near that location. The account of Corporal Amos Barrett, a member of Captain David Brown's Concord Minute Man Company, seems to support Governor Brooks' recollection of British casualties at Meriam's Corner. According to Barrett:

"After a while we found them a marching back toward Boston, we was soon after them. When they got about mil half to a road that comes from Bedford and Bildraa they was way laid and grait many killed when I got thair a great many lay dead and the road was bloddy."[18]

Barrett's account, which was written some 50 years or so after the event, is not supported by the account of Thaddeus Blood,

---

[16] Sumner, pp. 355-356.

[17] Ibid.

[18] Allen French, The Concord Fight, "An Account by Amos Barrett," Thomas Todd Co., Boston, 1924, p. 14.

an eyewitness to the Meriam's Corner exchange of fire. According to Blood's account, which was also written many years after the fact:

"Col. Thomeson of Billerica came up with 3 or 4 hundred men and there was a heavey fire but the distance so great, that little injury was done on either side, at least I saw but one killed, number wounded I know not."[19]

Blood's account correlates well with Ensign Lister's account of the colonials' opening fire coming from too great a range to be effective at Meriam's Corner. Blood, from his position near Deacon Minot's, would have been in a good position to observe the events that occurred at Meriam's Corner. Amos Barrett, on the other hand, reached Meriam's Corner shortly after the fighting as his minute company (Captain Brown's) apparently followed the British from the Concord Center area along the main road.

It must be remembered that the accounts of the Rev. Foster, John Brooks, Amos Barrett, and Thaddeus Blood were based on the recollections of old men a half century or more after the fight. To expect them to agree as to minute detail is to ask too much of human nature. The accounts of the British officers, Sutherland and Lister, on the other hand, are the accounts of young men writing much nearer in time to the events in question. Lt. Sutherland's account was written only a week after April 19, 1775, while Ensign Lister's account was written in 1782 based on his recollections of only seven years earlier. After considering the accounts of these professional officers, which are generally supported in regard to casualties by the later American account of the Rev. Edmund Foster and militia man Thaddeus Blood, this writer concluded that only a few British soldiers, probably two, were killed at Meriam's Corner. The number of British wounded there is uncertain, but the figure is probably not high. As to American casualties at Meriam's Corner, Lt. Sutherland's statement that two "villians" were killed in that location is not

---

[19] Blood, p. 3.

supported by any other evidence that this writer has seen. The historical record is also silent concerning American wounded at Meriam's Corner. This writer must conclude that few, if any, Americans were wounded at Meriam's Corner.

William Sumner's account of his recollection of Governor Brooks' statement concerning nine British soldiers found "hors de combat" at Meriam's corner and Amos Barrett's statement that "a great many lay dead and the road was bloddy," cannot be totally disregarded, even though they were made years after the fact by old men. Perhaps, the aged gentlemen included British casualties, which occurred along the road eastward of Meriam's Corner with those killed at that location.

As to who fired first at Meriam's Corner, one could make a good case on the available evidence that the colonials did. To do so, however, one would have to conclude that the Rev. Edmund Foster was in error when he said that the British fired first by facing about suddenly and firing a volley after they passed the small bridge. In many respects, the Rev. Foster's account is the most concise, and certainly the most graphic account we have concerning the opening fire at Meriam's Corner. Moreover, Rev. Foster's account did not offend the Rev. Ezra Ripley, who used it in his book published only 52 years after the event in question, to describe the fight at Meriam's Corner. If the Rev. Foster's account conflicted with the body of Concord tradition that prevailed at the time, it is highly doubtful that the Rev. Ripley would have published it in 1827. On the other hand, writing only eight years later, historian Lemuel Shattuck gave the impression that the provincials attacked the British at Meriam's Corner.[20] Shattuck's version of the fighting in Concord on April 19, 1775 was criticized by contemporaries, such as the Acton historian Josiah Adams. This writer has found that a number of Mr. Shattuck's statements concerning the details of the April 19, 1775 fighting are not supported by the existing documentation, although his overall story of that fateful day is correct.

---

[20] Shattuck, P. 114.

In relation to who fired first at Meriam's Corner, it is interesting to note that the Americans in their original depositions to the Second Provincial Congress between April 23 and 25, 1775, never accused the British of firing first, as they did at Lexington Common and Concord's North Bridge. In fact, the depositions are silent on the subject, and it didn't appear to be a matter of much controversy to the early nineteenth century historians. The Rev. Ezra Ripley was content to let the letter of Rev. Foster speak for him, while Mr. Shattuck indicated that the British were attacked at Meriam's Corner by the provincials who had crossed the Great Fields in conjunction with the Reading Company. The Acton historian Josiah Adams was not happy with Mr. Shattuck's account of Meriam's Corner, but he adds nothing to our knowledge of that particular point in the battle.

In the final analysis of who fired first at Meriam's Corner, either the Rev. Edmund Foster is correct is his statement that the British did or Ensign Lister, Lt. Sutherland, and Captain John Brooks (as retold by William Sumner), are correct in their version that the Americans opened fire first. If the British first opened the firing at Meriam's Corner, the American return fire was simply another response to British initiative, as was their fire at the North Bridge. On the other hand, if Captain Brooks ordered his men to fire on the British first, the firing of the Reading Company marked the first organized American offensive action on April 19, 1775.

In any event, Meriam's Corner marked the start of that galling American fire, which played havoc on the hard-pressed British column as it marched eastwards toward its haven in Boston.

5 - MERIAM'S CORNER THROUGH LINCOLN

As the rear of the British column passed the little bridge at Meriam's Corner, they probably left two dead privates behind. A few British had also received wounds at Meriam's Corner, including Ensign Jeremy Lister, whose right arm was disabled by a musket ball through his elbow. At this point, the British casualties for the day were still small in number, but the main danger was not far ahead of them.

The road immediately to the east of Meriam's Corner was built up into a causeway due to the low lying land on each side. This land was probably wet in the spring of 1775. The land soon rose, however, in a gradual incline, which crested about one mile eastward of Meriam's Corner. This hill is most often referred to as Hardy's Hill, but at least one contemporary account referred to it as Brook's Hill.

In his account, the Reverend Ezra Ripley referred to a company from East Sudbury as being at Meriam's Corner on the south side of the road. This could have been Captain Joseph Smith's 50-man militia company. According to Sudbury tradition, as repeated by the town's historian, Alfred S. Hudson, the 40-

man minute company of Captain Nathaniel Cudworth attacked the British vigorously at Hardy's Hill.[1]

As the historical record is silent concerning the role of Sudbury at Meriam's Corner, it is quite possible that Smith's company moved eastward to join Cudworth's minute company in the attack on the British at Hardy's Hill. It is also possible that other units from Sudbury's six companies joined the ambush at Hardy's Hill. Captain John Nixon's minute company, for example, suffered casualties that could have occurred on Hardy's Hill or further to the east. Unfortunately, detailed information concerning Sudbury's role in the battle is not clear.

There is one account by the British Lieutenant William Sutherland which may describe the fighting on Hardy's Hill. Due to the breast wound he received at Concord's North Bridge, Sutherland was riding in an enclosed one-horse chaise. The position of this chaise in the British column is unknown, but it could have been more forward than to the rear. According to Lt. Sutherland: "just to the end of the town next to this a few concealed villians fired on us, of which we killed 2, but they wounded 2 of ours..."[2]

Sutherland's account could also, of course, refer to the fighting at Meriam's Corner or even from Deacon Minot's farm where the Concord militia man, Thaddeus Blood, had taken up an ambush position. The American firing at Meriam's Corner, however, came from a larger body of men than the "few concealed villians" Sutherland mentions. It also killed two British soldiers and wounded more. Sudbury had two men killed on April 19th and one wounded. One of the men killed, Asahel Reed, and the wounded man, Joshua Haynes, Jr., may have been casualties of the Hardy's Hill fighting. In any case, when Sutherland's preceding statement is considered in context with

---

[1] Alfred S. Hudson, The History of Sudbury Massachusetts, published by the Town of Sudbury, Sudbury, 1889, p. 380.

[2] Vincent J. R. Kehoe, We Were There! The British Soldiers, "Lt. Wm. Sutherland's Letter to Henry Clinton, April 26, 1775," p. 143.

his account which follows and with other accounts, it is more appropriate to Hardy's Hill than Meriam's Corner. Former National Park Service historian, Robert Ronsheim, held this view, although the Concord historian, Allen French, felt Sutherland was describing the Meriam's Corner action.

From a close reading of Lt. Sutherland's account, it would appear that the British had heavy flanking parties out along the stretch of road leading up Hardy's Hill. In fact, according to Sutherland, the British were able to prevent the men who had attacked them at the bridge at Meriam's Corner from joining a large body of men who had drawn up on Sutherland's left.[3] Flankers could only delay the colonials who had exchanged fire with the British at Meriam's Corner for a short time. As the British column moved eastward, so did the flankers, and there was nothing to prevent the colonials from following them on the road or through the adjacent fields.

According to Chelmsford tradition, the companies of Captain Oliver Barron and Colonel (Acting Captain) Moses Parker first engaged the British at Meriam's Corner and later at Hardy's Hill. It was at Hardy's Hill, according to the tradition, that Sergeant John Ford of Captain Barron's 61-man Chelmsford company displayed great bravery. Ford is said to have killed five British soldiers before the day's fighting was over.[4] According to Frederic Hudson, the Sudbury company of Captain Nathaniel Cudworth also attacked the British at Hardy's Hill.[5] Hudson does not mention any other Sudbury companies as joining Cudworth's company in the attack, but it is quite possible that others were there including the East Sudbury militia company commanded by Captain Joseph Smith. It is possible that the Sudbury forces enjoyed the support of men from Framingham's three companies

---

[3] Ibid.

[4] Samuel Adams Drake, History of Middlesex County, Vol. I, Estes and Lauriat, Boston, 1880, p. 375.

[5] Frederic Hudson, Harper's New Monthly Magazine, No. 300, May, 1875, Vol. L, "The Concord Fight," Harper and Brothers, New York, 1875, p. 801.

at Hardy's Hill, but it is not clear if Framingham first struck the British in force at this location.

Despite Lt. Sutherland's statement that the colonials who attacked the British at the bridge at Meriam's Corner were prevented from joining the large colonial force on his left flank, it appears that some companies did get into a position to do damage to the British on Hardy's Hill. The Chelmsford companies were, of course, with the group of Middlesex companies who engaged the British at Meriam's Corner. It is quite probable that companies from such towns as Reading and Billerica were also able to catch up with the moving British column in the Hardy's Hill area. In this writer's opinion, the colonial companies from Meriam's Corner probably engaged the rear of the British column, but would have had difficulty in engaging the King's troops marching in the more forward positions of the long column.

In any event, the historical record concerning the action on Hardy's Hill remains clouded. It is doubtful, however, if many casualties were inflicted on either side during this stretch of the road. Eastward of Hardy's Hill, the terrain and cover offered the Provincials a better opportunity to wait within musket range in concealed ambush positions.

As the British column passed over the crest of Hardy's Hill, the road descended to a bridge, which spanned a brook called Elm or Tanner's Brook. The road then climbed eastward into Lincoln where it made a deep cut through the hill as it bent sharply to the northeast. Some 50 years later, the Reverend Edmund Foster wrote an account of the action which most historians relate to this area. Foster was serving as a private in Captain John Brooks' Reading Minute Company and was an eyewitness to the following scene he described in his letter to Colonel Daniel Shattuck of Concord, dated March 10, 1825.

"We saw a wood at a distance, which appeared to be in or near the road the enemy must pass. Many leaped over the wall and made for that wood. We arrived just in time to meet the enemy. There was then, on the opposite side of the road, a young growth of wood well filled with Americans. The

enemy was now completely between two fires, renewed and briskly kept up. They ordered out a flank guard on the left to dislodge the Americans from their posts behind large trees: but they only became a better mark to be shot at. A short but sharp contest ensued, at which the enemy received more deadly injury, than at any one place from Concord to Charlestown. Eight or more of their number were killed on the spot, and no doubt, many wounded."[6]

Most historians relate the preceding description by the Rev. Foster to the stretch of road in Lincoln that came to be called locally the "Bloody Angle." There is some uncertainty today concerning the exact location of the "Bloody Angle." Some think that the "Angle" represents the area near the road's first sharp bend to the northeast in Lincoln, as one proceeds east from Concord. Other historians feel that the "Bloody Angle" refers to the second sharp angle the road makes as it bends back to the east. Another point of view holds that the so called "Bloody Angle" should include the area included by both the sharp bends. From a close study of the eyewitness accounts, it is impossible to determine the exact point in which the fighting was the heaviest and the most blood spilled.

In any event, by the time the British had reached the stretch of road in Lincoln, the battle had assumed the character of a running ambush. According to the Rev. Edmund Foster's description of the fighting east of Meriam's Corner:

"The battle now began, and was carried on with little or no military discipline and order, on the part of the Americans, during the remainder of that day. Each one sought his own place and opportunity to attack and annoy the enemy from behind trees, rocks, fences, and buildings, as seemed most convenient."[7]

---

[6] Rev. Ezra Ripley, D. C, <u>A History of the Fight at Concord, on the 19th of April, 1775</u>, Allen and Atwill, Concord, 1827, pp. 33-34.

[7] Ibid., p. 33.

The popular theme often heard about the fighting on April 19, 1775 is that the British marched stupidly down the road in their brilliant red uniforms, while clever Yankee sharp shooters picked them off like turkeys from their concealed positions in the brush. This myth is misleading. To begin with, the 18th century smooth bore flintlock musket was not a weapon noted for its accuracy. With such a weapon, a soldier was lucky to hit the man he aimed at beyond a range of 80 yards. Moreover, the British column formation was not a poor choice. It provided good firepower to the flanks and provided a fast way to move a large body of troops through generally unfamiliar territory. In addition, the British officers tried to keep their flankers well out, so as to keep the colonials beyond the effective musket range of the main body of troops marching in the road. The vigorous activity of the Light Infantry flankers would save many a British life between Meriam's Corner in Concord and Bunker Hill in Charlestown. The flankers would also account for a high percentage of the Americans killed as the day wore on.

The flankers could not prevent, however, the men who engaged the British at Meriam's Corner from catching up to them again in Lincoln; as the Rev. Foster, then serving as a private in the Reading Minute Man Company, recalled, "We arrived just in time to meet the enemy."[8] The progress of the British column, of course, must have been slowed somewhat by the sharp bend in the road to the northeast. Even so, the Reading men had to hustle through the fields on the south side of the road in order to catch up with the British. The older and slower men of the colonial companies must have fell behind as they cut through the fields between Meriam's Corner and the "Bloody Angle" area. To the Rev. Foster it appeared that company organization had broken down as the men arrived and sought their individual ambush positions.

The Reading men were not the only ones to catch up with the British in the "Bloody Angle" area. Men from Bedford, Billerica, Chelmsford, and other towns probably had time to cut across the

---

[8] Ibid.

fields from Meriam's Corner to ambush positions in the "Bloody Angle" area on the left side of the road. The Rev. Foster's account indicated that there were large trees on this side of the road, which the Provincials utilized for cover. According to the Reverend's account, the British tried to dislodge these colonials with their flank guard, but the flankers only succeeded in making better targets for the colonials to aim at.[9]

The Rev. Foster also mentioned that there was a young growth of wood on the opposite side of the road that was "well filled with Americans."[10] Shortly after he passed the Meriam's Corner area, Lt. Sutherland wrote that he saw:

"Upon a height to my right hand a vast number of armed men drawn out in Battalia order, I dare say near 1000 who on our coming nearer dispersed into the woods, & came as close to the road on our flanking partys as they possibly could, upon our ascending the height to the road gave us a very heavy fire, but some shot from the left hand drew my attention that way when I saw a much larger body drawn up to my left, this I take to be the party with whom those that attacked us at the Bridge meant to join & which we fortunately prevented..."[11]

According to the former historian at Minute Man National Historical Park, Robert Ronsheim, Lt. Sutherland would have seen the next hill straight ahead and to his right as he passed Samuel Brooks' house and started his descent of the east side of Hardy's Hill. According to Ronsheim, the large formation Sutherland saw in battalion order must have been the Woburn men and others.[12] This writer is in accord with Ronsheim on this point.

---

[9] Ibid., p. 34.

[10] Ibid., pp. 33-34.

[11] Kehoe, The British Soldiers, "Lt. Sutherland's Letter to Sir Henry Clinton," p. 143.

[12] Robert D. Ronsheim, "Troop Movement Map: Narrative Section," February 1964 (unpublished report in the files of Minute Man National Historical Park), p. 20.

According to Woburn's Loammi Baldwin, his town was alerted by an express from Cambridge shortly before daybreak that the British were on the move to Concord. The thirty-one year old Baldwin mustered with his men and then rode a little before the main body of the Woburn forces. Baldwin is not recorded among the 256 names Frank Warren Coburn lists in the three Woburn companies that responded on April 19, 1775. According to the historian William R. Cutter, Loammi Baldwin held a rank equivalent to that of major on April 19.[13] Baldwin had prior military experience, as in 1768 he had enlisted in "His Excellency's Troop of Horse Guards" under the command of Colonel David Phips. He was also descended from one of the oldest, and influential families of Woburn.[14]

In the spring of 1775, Woburn could be included among the many Massachusetts towns that had foreseen a conflict with the British Army as a distinct possibility. As early as December 23, 1773, at a general town meeting the townsmen voted to build a house in which to store their ammunition. Moreover, they had appointed a committee to procure an additional two barrels of powder, as well as more bullets and flints. In addition, they later directed their constable to pay the tax money raised in Woburn to Henry Gardner, Esquire of Stow, instead of Harrison Gray, Esquire, who had been appointed the preceding year by the General Court.[15] In short, Woburn supported the Provincial Congress and not the Tory-dominated colonial government headed by General Thomas Gage.

As Woburn did not vote to form minute man companies until April 17, 1775, the three companies that followed Baldwin into Concord two days later were probably marching under the designation of militia. The three Woburn companies were under

---

[13] D. Hamilton Hurd, History of Middlesex County Massachusetts, Vol. I, J. W. Lewis & Co., Philadelphia, 1890, p. 390.

[14] Ibid, pp. 446-447.

[15] Samuel Sewall, M. A., The History of Woburn, Wiggin and Lunt, Publishers, Boston, 1868, pp. 360-361.

the direct command of Captains Samuel Belknap, Jonathan Fox, and Joshua Walker. Coburn's muster rolls indicate that Captain Walker's company was under the regimental command of Colonel David Green of the 2nd Regiment of Foot in the County of Middlesex. Coburn's rolls indicate 256 officers and men as seeing service from Woburn on April 19, 1775. According to the September 20, 1775 deposition of William Tay, Jr. (who is probably the Will Tay Coburn lists as a member of Captain Jonathan Fox's company), he and 180 of his fellow townsmen marched to Concord by way of Lexington, where they were "deeply touched" by the results that had occurred on and near Lexington Common. In his deposition, Tay said that upon his arrival in Concord, his force of 180 men was reinforced with a number of fellow soldiers from the same regiment.[16] Frank Coburn, during his search of the State archives, found 256 names enrolled in the three Woburn companies. It is possible that some of the Woburn men Coburn included in his rolls reported later in the day or joined the Woburn companies during the encampment at Cambridge that followed the fighting.

In any event, after viewing the bodies of the eight slain Lexington militiamen, the Woburn men continued their march through Lexington and Lincoln and passed over the border into Concord. Apparently, Major Baldwin had stopped at one of the houses near the Concord and Lincoln line for refreshment. He was probably in one of the Brooks' houses that sat on either side of the road. The following remarks are taken from Major Baldwin's diary entry for April 19, 1775:

"We proceeded to Concord by way of Lincoln meeting-house...ascended the hill and pitched and refreshed ourselves a little... The people under my command and also some others came running off the East end of the hill while I was at a house...and we proceeded down the road and could see behind us the Regulars following. We came to Tanner Brook, at Lincoln

---

[16] Richard Frothingham, History of the Siege of Boston, Little Brown and Company, Boston, 1896, p. 368.

Bridge, and then concluded to scatter and make use of the trees and walls for to defend us, and attack them...[17]

From Major Baldwin's account it is clear that the three Woburn companies reversed their direction upon sight of the British column marching eastward from Meriam's Corner. The Woburn men accompanied by "some others" went back down the hill leading to Elm or Tanner's Brook. It is not clear who the men were who accompanied the Woburn companies at this point, but they could have been men from Sudbury or Framingham. Shortly after passing Elm Brook, the Woburn men and the others scattered into the woods to utilize the trees and walls as cover. They probably climbed the hill to take advantage of the high ground east of Elm Brook. As noted earlier, the road eastward of Elm Brook climbed the hill where it bent sharply through a cut in the land to the northeast in Lincoln. It is generally thought that the Woburn companies along with men from Framingham's two minute and one militia company took up ambush positions that put them on the British right flank. Some of them may have taken up positions on the other side of the road as well. In any event, other militia and minute companies had taken up or were hurrying toward ambush positions on the British left flank, or the westerly side of the road along the stretch where it runs for about 3/10 of a mile to the northeast. In short, the unfortunate British column would soon be taken under heavy fire from both sides of the road.

It should be noted that at this point the Americans were no longer waiting for the British to fire first as they had done earlier in the day. The memory of the eight fallen militiamen of Lexington, whose bodies they had viewed as they passed through that town, must have been fresh in the minds of the Woburn men as they carefully chose their ambush positions.

According to the Framingham tradition, as repeated by historian Josiah Temple in his history of that town, Framingham's two minute and one militia company were all

---

[17] Hurd, p. 447.

active in the fighting that took place in the "Lincoln woods."[18] As the muster rolls indicate that they reached Concord on the morning of the 19th, it is quite possible that they, like the Woburn companies, reversed direction upon the sight of the British and, perhaps in company with Woburn, proceeded eastward across the Lincoln line to take up ambush positions in the "Bloody Angle" area. It should be noted that there is a Framingham tradition that some of that town's men were present during the exchange of fire at Meriam's Corner. They are not mentioned at that location by the Rev. Ripley or Lemuel Shattuck, but it is possible that some Framingham men from Captain Micajah Gleason's company arrived in Concord ahead of the main force from that town. According to Temple, those Framingham men living on the extreme south and west sides of the town were a little behind the party from the center and north side of town.[19]

The Framingham minute companies had formed on December 2, 1774. Each man was ordered to provide himself with a musket, bayonet, cartridge box, and 36 rounds of ammunition. During the winter they met for drills at the homes of their officers. Temple quoted one of them as saying "I have spent many an evening, with a number of my near neighbors, going through the exercises in the barn floor, with my mittons on."[20]

Captain Simon Edgell was forty-two years old when he commanded his large 76-man minute company on April 19, 1775. He, like Captain Micajah Gleason, who commanded the town's smaller 49-man minute company, were both veterans of the earlier French and Indian War. (According to Temple, Thomas Nixon commanded one of the two Framingham minute

[18] Josiah H. Temple, History of Framingham Massachusetts, published by the Town of Framingham, Framingham, 1887, p. 274.

[19] Ibid.

[20] Ibid, p. 269.

companies, but Coburn's muster rolls indicate that Gleason commanded the smaller minute man unit.) Framingham's 24-man militia company, according to Coburn's rolls, was commanded by Captain Jesse Ernes. Coburn's rolls indicate that 149 men saw service with Framingham's three companies on April 19th. On the other hand, Temple claimed that 153 men from Framingham marched against the King's troops on the first day of the war.

Peter Salem, who had spent years in slavery, was one of the minute men assigned to Captain Edgell's minute company. Later in June during the battle known as Bunker Hill, Salem would gain some fame as the man who fired the fatal musket ball into Major John Pitcairn.[21]

It should be noted that in 1775 many black people in Massachusetts were held in legal bondage. As slaves, they were excluded from military service unless their masters granted permission for them to enlist. As most masters did not wish to risk the lives and limbs of their valuable labor force in the dangerous undertaking of warfare, blacks were a distinct minority among the colonials who fought the British on April 19, 1775. Exceptions to this rule besides Peter Salem were Prince Estabrook, who was wounded at Lexington with Captain John Parker's company, Cato Stedman and Cato Boardman of Captain Samuel Thatcher's Cambridge militia company, a man listed as Josha, Boylston's Prince, who served in Captain Thomas White's Brookline militia company, Cuff Whittemore and Cato Wood of Captain Benjamin Locke's Menotomy Company, and Caesar Baron of Captain Jonathan Minot's Westford Militia Company.[22] David Lamson, apparently of mixed race and not attached to any organized unit, was one of the leaders in the attack on Lord

---

[21] Ibid, pp. 324-325.

[22] Frank Warren Coburn, The Battle of April 19, 1775 in Lexington, Concord, Lincoln, Arlington, Cambridge, Somerville and Charlestown, Massachusetts, F. L. Coburn and Co., Boston, 1912, pp. 5-76.

Percy's supply wagons in Menotomy.[23] There were probably others as well whose identity has gone unrecorded.

Later in the war when white enlistments began to lag, free blacks were encouraged to enlist in the Continental Army and various state regiments. Slaves could also enlist in many states with their owner's permission. As a reward for their military service, they were granted their freedom. Peter Salem of Framingham was one of many blacks who obtained his freedom in this manner. Salem reenlisted several times throughout the war and survived to live the remainder of his life as a free man.[24]

In any event, as the British column made their turn to the northeast in Lincoln they came under the guns of the minute and militia men on both sides of the road. It is unclear as to whether the colonials attacked the head of the column or at some point behind the leading elements. They may have withheld their fire until the leading troops were beyond the northeast turn, as by crouching low the British soldiers would have had some protection from the walls that bordered the stretch of road that had been cut out of the hillside at the road's curve. What is clear is that the British came under heavy fire from the Woburn men and others on each side of the road. Moreover, their flanking force could not keep the colonial fire off the main force in the road. As the Rev. Foster indicated in his account, the flank guard on the left became marks for the Reading Company which, after hurrying from Meriam's Corner, had just arrived on the scene of ambush.

As noted earlier, the road ran about 3/10 of a mile to the northeast from the point of its turn in Lincoln until it bent to the southeast. According to the Rev. Foster's account, there were large trees to the left of the road and a young growth of wood on the opposite side which was well filled with Americans.[25] The

[23] Allen French, The Day of Concord and Lexington, Little, Brown and Company, Boston, 1925, footnote, p. 230.

[24] Temple, pp. 324-325.

[25] Ripley, pp. 33-34.

woody nature of the terrain in the area was also noted by Major Loammi Baldwin, who stated that his men scattered and made use of trees and walls as cover for their ambush.[26] The fact Baldwin's men scattered may indicate that the trees were not dense and the men had to disperse in order to find cover. In this area the British suffered perhaps the most effective fire they would receive along any stretch of the road that fateful day.

How many Americans and the towns they represented that engaged the British along this portion of the road in unclear. It appears certain that they were engaged by sizable contingents from Woburn, Framingham, Reading, Billerica, Chelmsford, and Bedford. It is also likely that Westford and Stow were able to catch up to the British at this point. As the British column moved eastward, men from Sudbury may have also exchanged fire with the British along this stretch of road. Certainly many of the men who had engaged the British at the North Bridge earlier had also pursued them this far and would pursue them even further as the battle moved eastward.

Firing from behind trees and walls the Americans had the British soldiers at a disadvantage. Trained in the open field lineal warfare prevalent in Europe at the time, the average British soldier had a hard time coping with the type of tactics the Massachusetts men employed. In fact, many of the King's troops considered the colonials cowards for firing at them from prone positions and from behind cover. The British flankers tried to deal with the situation the best they could, but they failed to keep the main column from coming under heavy attack. How many British were killed or wounded in the short stretch of road from the point it bent to the northeast to the point it turned to the southeast is unclear. Perhaps the figure of eight killed that is given in the Rev. Edmund Foster's account is fairly accurate.[27] The Rev. Foster also stated that many were wounded, which seems entirely likely considering the heavy fire the British received in this area.

---

[26] Hurd, p. 447.

[27] Ripley, p. 34.

As the road bent to the southeast it passed the farms of Joseph Mason, Ephraim Hartwell, Samuel Hartwell, and Captain William Smith. The farmhouses of these Lincoln men were located on the north side of the road on the British left flank. The land was more open here and, except for the farm structures and perhaps orchards on the opposite side of the road, this area probably provided the New England men with less cover to fire from than the stretch of road which preceded it. The firing in the Hartwell neighborhood was less intense than it had been at the "Bloody Angle." Nevertheless, the British and colonials received casualties in the vicinity of the two Hartwell Farms.

One of the men killed in the Hartwell area was Captain Jonathan Wilson of the Bedford Minute Men. Wilson apparently ate breakfast earlier in the morning at the tavern in Bedford kept by Jeremiah Fitch, Jr. According to an old Bedford tradition, Wilson remarked at breakfast, "It is a cold breakfast boys, but we'll give the British a hot one,--we'll have every dog of them before night."[28] According to the Rev. Ripley, Captain Wilson was killed with others behind a barn by the British flankers. The Rev. Ripley did not identify the barn except to say that it was little farther on from that location where the road bent to the north and the heavy action occurred. He also said that it was near the close of the action which occurred at the large bend to the north.[29] Lemuel Shattuck, however, is more specific than the Rev. Ripley and recorded that Captain Wilson, along with Nathaniel Wyman of Billerica and Daniel Thompson of Woburn, was killed in or close by Mr. Hartwell's barn.[30] Unfortunately, Mr. Shattuck did not indicate which Hartwell Barn was the scene of their deaths.

In his book Beneath Old Roof Trees, Abram English Brown recorded an old Woburn tradition relating to the death of Daniel

[28] Drake, p. 244.

[29] Ripley, p. 31.

[30] Shattuck, p. 115.

Thompson of that town. According to this tradition, Thompson stepped behind a barn to load, then aiming from the corner of the building, he fired diagonally through the ranks of the enemy, thus "making every shot effectual." As the traditional story goes, a grenadier noticed Thompson's dangerous activity, ran around the other corner of the barn, and shot Thompson dead while the latter was in the act of reloading. According to this tradition, the grenadier was then shot by another Woburn man, who some say was one of Thompson's two brothers who were also present at the scene.[31]

In addition to Captain Jonathan Wilson, who was the second colonial militia officer to be killed in the Revolutionary War, Job Lane, also of Bedford, was severely wounded in the Lincoln engagement and disabled for life. Lane, along with his dead captain, was carried back to Bedford by some of his comrades in arms, while others from Bedford went in pursuit of the British. They would encamp that night in Cambridge.[32]

According to the Rev. Ripley's account, Captain Wilson and others were killed by flankers behind a barn. The old Woburn tradition, on the other hand, mentioned that Daniel Thompson had been killed by a grenadier who noticed him by the barn and went after him. The consensus view of April 19 holds that the grenadiers were marching on the road at this point of the battle and that the light infantry was out on the flanks. If a grenadier did kill Thompson, it is quite possible that he left the road on his own initiative after spotting Thompson by the side of the barn. In any event, the British flankers would end the life of many a Massachusetts man before the day would end. The concentration of many Provincials was so directed at the King's troops in the road that they didn't notice the flanking parties sweeping through the backyards and fields that paralleled the road. They paid the ultimate price for their inexperience, as so often happens in war.

---

[31] Abram English Brown, Beneath Old Roof Trees, Lee and Shepard, Boston, 1896, p. 314.

[32] Ibid, p. 177.

It is also interesting to note the mix of men from the three towns, Bedford, Billerica, and Woburn, that were killed in the vicinity of Hartwell's barn. Does this indicate that company organization had broken down among the Americans at this point and that the Provincial companies were mixed in together? It is also interesting to note that Woburn's Daniel Thompson was killed on the north side of the road. The consensus view of historians is that the Woburn companies engaged the British from ambush positions on the British right. The fact that Thompson was killed on the British left flank indicates that at least he, if not others from Woburn, crossed over the road prior to the British arrival along the stretch.

At this point, the traditional story, as related by Mary Hartwell to her grandchildren and repeated in Abram English Brown's <u>Beneath Old Roof Trees</u> should be mentioned. Mary, of course, was the wife of the Lincoln Minute Man Sergeant Samuel Hartwell. Sam and Mary lived with their children in the next house to the east of Samuel's father Ephraim. Mary witnessed the return passage of the British troops from her home on the north side of the road. Her description of the British passage was printed by Brown in 1896 as follows:

"I saw an occasional horseman dashing by, going up and down, but heard nothing more until I saw them coming back in the afternoon, all in confusion, wild with rage, and loud with threats. I knew there had been trouble, and that it had not resulted favorably for that retreating army. I heard the musket-shots just below, by the old Brook's Tavern, and trembled, believing that our folks were killed. Some of the rough, angry soldiers rushed up to this house and fired in; but fortunately for me and the children, the shots went into the garret, and we were safe. How glad I was when they all got by the house, and your grandfather and our neighbors reached home alive!"[33]

The British appeared to show a special interest in the Samuel Hartwell house. Did they fire into the garret because they saw an

---

[33] Ibid, p. 221.

actual sniper on the upper level, or was it simple suppression fire to discourage any potential snipers who might have been lurking within the upstairs rooms? It seems unlikely that any of the militia were upstairs or Mary would have mentioned them in her account to her grandchildren.

In Volume III of her work entitled The Beginnings of the American Revolution, Ellen Chase related a somewhat different version of British activity at the Samuel Hartwell house. According to this version, a detail of soldiers was ordered to burn Hartwell's house, as the Tories wanted revenge on Samuel Hartwell for the services he had rendered the Patriot cause as a gunsmith. As the story went, the soldiers were too closely pressed to carry out their instructions and only succeeded in sending a few bullets through the windows. One soldier, however, according to this tale, thrust a damaged musket into a window and let it slip from his grip. According to this account, Sergeant Samuel Hartwell found the musket upon his return, repaired it, and used it in later years when he went hunting.[34]

As the British column moved eastward past Samuel Hartwell's house, they would pass by the home of Captain William Smith of the Lincoln Minute Men. The fighting along the stretch of the road was probably far less intense than it had been earlier near the two sharp bends in the road. Nevertheless, a badly wounded grenadier was left along the roadside near William Smith's house by his hard-pressed companions. At some point in time after the British column had cleared the neighborhood, the mortally wounded soldier was carried inside Captain William Smith's home. According to the Lincoln tradition, the wounded man was cared for by a woman until he died within three or four days. He was probably nursed by the family slave under the directions of and aided by Mrs. Smith. According to this tradition, the soldier, feeling life slipping from his body, asked the "maid" who cared for him to look in his coat-lining, where she could keep the gold sovereign concealed

---

[34] Ellen Chase, The Beginnings of the American Revolution, Vol. III, Sir Isaac Pitman and Sons, Ltd. London, 1911, p. 66.

there. At first, the coin could not be found, but after this soldier's death Mrs. Smith succeeded in finding it. Apparently the last days of the unfortunate grenadier's life had been miserable, as he had implored those caring for him to terminate his pain by ending his life. He was buried in a field a little west of Folly Pond in Lincoln.[35]

The above account of the luckless grenadier was published by Ellen Chase in 1911. According to Frank Coburn, the remains of a British soldier were found in the late 19th century when workmen were widening and grading anew the highway near Folly Pond. The remains were reinterred over the wall in the field southwest of the road, a short distance west of Folly Pond. Coburn stated that a nearby resident, Mr. George Nelson, who saw the remains in 1890, pointed out to him the locations of the old and new graves.[36] At the time of this writing, the exact location of this unmarked grave is unknown to this author.

It should be noted that many of the British who were killed on April 19, 1775 were buried in unmarked graves in the fields bordering the road of battle. The exact locations of many of these graves are unknown to us today, although we know the general area in which a number of these unfortunate men were laid to rest. Not all of them were buried beside the road. Five of the British soldiers killed in Lincoln, not far from the Hartwell houses, were transported in an ox cart to the old burying ground in Lincoln, where they were interred in a common grave. They had lain in the dusty road overnight until, according to an account attributed to Mary Hartwell by A. E. Brown:

"The men hitched the oxen to the cart and went down below the house, and gathered up the dead. As they returned with the team and the dead soldiers, my thoughts went out for the wives, parents, and children away across the Atlantic, who would never again see their loved ones. And I left the house, and taking my little children by the hand, I followed the rude

---

[35] Ibid, p. 67.

[36] Coburn, p. 103.

hearse to the grave hastily made in the burial-ground. I remember how cruel it seemed to put them into one large trench without any coffins. There was one in a brilliant uniform whom I supposed to be an officer. His hair was tied up in a cue."[37]

According to Frank Hersey's version of the preceding story, Mary in later years remarked that she was the first, and only, mourner of the fallen enemy. According to Hersey, the young officer Mary noted in Brown's preceding account had been killed at the "Bloody Angle." Hersey further stated that this young officer had "lay in the dust the whole afternoon, his head pillowed on the broad black ribbons of his queue, and his ruffled shirt gleaming in the sunlight."[38] According to Hersey, it was old Ephraim Hartwell and another elderly man who picked the five bodies up and transported them to the Lincoln burying ground in the ox cart. Strenuous work for the sixty-eight year old Hartwell and his elderly companion, but New England farmers were a hardy lot.

As the British passed beyond the Smith House, Folly Pond was located on their right. The British ranks had been thinned a bit and there were a number of wounded men, who must have found it difficult to keep with the column without help from their able-bodied comrades in arms.

The British followed the road as it passed north of Folly Pond and soon found themselves in the neighborhood where the Nelson Family had erected their homes. There were two fields on the northerly side of the road. The first field contained a number of trenches, and the second field contained a great many boulders of various sizes and shapes. According to Ellen Chase, a Lincoln man was firing at the British from the first field when he became hemmed in between the British flank guard and the main body of troops in the road. The flankers fired at him but,

---

[37] Brown, p. 226.

[38] Frank Wilson Cheney Hersey, <u>Heroes of the Battle Road,</u> Perry Walton, Boston, 1930, p. 25.

according to Chase, the man dropped down into one of a number of trenches in the field and the musket balls passed over him. When the flankers moved out of the area, the Lincoln man rose and took up a position behind a large boulder in the second field, which is located on the north side of the road just east of Josiah Nelson's house. According to Chase, the Lincoln man used the rock as a gun-rest and fired several more shots at the British.[39]

Ellen Chase apparently obtained the information for the above story from an article in the April 18, 1900 edition of the Boston Evening Transcript. Frank Coburn's book, which was printed a year later than Chase's 1911 three volume work, names the Lincoln man as William Thorning, who is listed as a minute man in Captain William Smith's company. Coburn stated that Thorning fired from the field "probably with fatal effect" and that two soldiers are buried in the little knoll across the road. According to Coburn, the British graves were pointed out to him in 1890 by George Nelson, a descendent of Josiah Nelson.[40]

Frank Hersey in his Heroes of the Battle Road, printed in 1930, definitely states that Thorning killed two British soldiers from his position behind the rock in the boulder-strewn field. He also stated that they were buried on a knoll across the road. He further identified the gravesite as being in an orchard southeast of the Nelson house.[41]

The stories of Chase, Coburn, and Hersey differ somewhat in detail, but they are similar in the main point that the British were fired on from the boulder-dotted field by a Lincoln man. Hersey, however, claims to have identified the boulder from which the fatal shots were fired, and published a picture of it in his 1930 publication. This boulder is presently known as "Minute Man Rock."

---

[39] Chase, Vol. III, p. 67.

[40] Coburn, pp. 103-104.

[41] Hersey, pp. 27-29.

Former Park Service Historian Robert Ronsheim and others have been troubled by Hersey's identification of the rock Thorning was said to have fired from, as it is located only 30 feet from the road. From a position so close to the road, Thorning would have been in great danger from the flanking parties and from the troops on the road as well. There is another rock some 40 or so feet further from the road than Hersey's that was still within effective musket range. It would seem more logical for Thorning to have chosen the rock more distant from the road where he could have fired with less danger to himself. Ronsheim pointed out also, however, that Thorning may have held his fire until the main body had passed and concentrated his aim at the rear of the main body or the stragglers who must have followed it.[42]

Ronsheim came to the conclusion that the core of the Thorning story had its origins in fact rather that fancy, but the conflicting details had to be accepted as traditional.[43] This writer shares Ronsheim's concern over the accuracy of the details of the Thorning story and the boulder identified by Hersey generally called "Minute Man Rock."

As the British passed Josiah Nelson's farmhouse, they neared the home of Thomas Nelson, Jr. located in Lincoln very near the Lexington line. According to tradition, one of the British soldiers entered the house intent on plunder. He was shot on the doorstep of the residence by a person whose name history does not record. According to Coburn, he was found seriously wounded by family members upon their return to the house later in the afternoon. According to this tradition, he was carried inside and his needs were ministered to as best as possible. Despite this kind attention, he died from his wound. After his death, a search of his pockets revealed a few of the family's silver

---

[42] Ronsheim, p. 25.

[43] Ibid.

spoons. His body was laid to rest in a location given by Coburn as "a short distance westerly from the house."[44]

It is unfortunate that the memory of this British soldier has been tarnished by the discovery of the spoons on his person. On stealing private property, this soldier was acting in direct disregard to General Gage's formal orders to Colonel Smith, which specifically forbade the plunder of the inhabitants. Whether Smith had time to stress the prohibition of looting to his officers is a matter of doubt due to the fast pace of events, which had occurred since the soldiers were first awakened in their Boston barracks. In any event, this soldier paid a stiff price for his temporary possession of a few silver spoons.

It should be remarked that Coburn was in error when he described the Thomas Nelson, Jr. house as that of a residence belonging to Samuel Hastings. The latter did not acquire title to the property until 1779. In 1775, Thomas Nelson, Jr. resided in the house with his wife Lydia, his daughter Lydia, and son Jonathan.[45]

As the head of the British column passed by the Thomas Nelson, Jr. house, they came to a small bridge, which Thomas Nelson, Sr. had erected at the Lincoln-Lexington line. Lincoln had not been kind to the British, and they had undergone the heaviest fire most of them had ever experienced in the last two miles. As he passed into Lexington, Colonel Smith must have wondered what was holding up the relief force he had requested. His eyes may have gazed apprehensively at the growth-covered ridge to his left. His force was still in great danger and he still had a long way to march through what was now enemy territory.

---

[44] Coburn, p. 104.

[45] David H. Snow, Archeological Research Report, Excavation at Site 264 The Thomas Nelson, Jr. House, Minute Man National Historical Park, Lincoln, Massachusetts, 1973, pp. 3-4, Minute Man National Historical Park Collection.

6 – MEETING WITH PERCY

Shortly after the van of the British column passed over the line from Lincoln into Lexington, the road ran by a growth covered ridge on the British left flank. According to the accepted tradition, Captain John Parker engaged the British in the area of the Lincoln-Lexington town line. The ridge was the most logical place in this area for the experienced Parker to set up an ambush. The high ground overlooked the road, which was within musket range, and its wild growth would have provided Captain Parker and his 120 or so men with some cover. The Cambridge Militia Company of 77 men under Captain Samuel Thatcher was also in this area and it could have acted in concert with Parker from an elevated position on the ridge.

In any case, thoughts of revenge must have been in the minds of the Lexington citizen-soldiers as they watched the van of the British column approach. Lexington in 1775 was a close-knit community. Many of the men killed or wounded by the British earlier in the day on Lexington Common were relatives of or well-known by the militiamen in Captain Parker's Company. For example, the rolls of the Lexington Militia Company include 16 Munroes, 13 Harringtons, 11 Smiths, and 8 Reeds.[1]

Major John R. Galvin in his book, The Minute Men, which was first published in 1967, provided considerable detail concerning Parker's ambush of the British in his chapter 21 entitled "Parker's Revenge." While Major Galvin's description of the "Parker's Revenge" incident is perhaps a brilliant, and certainly imaginative account of what may have happened, the documentation Major Galvin provided for his story does not support the depth of detail contained in his account. The early historian, Ezra Ripley, stated only that Captain Parker's company attacked the British within the bounds of Lexington from the woods on the south of the road.[2] Lemuel Shattuck made no reference to Parker's ambush while the Lexington Historian Elias Phinney recorded that Captain Parker's men gave the British a "galling and deadly fire" from a field in Lincoln.[3] Ellen Chase in her book published in 1911, repeated the Reverend Ripley's version of the story. In addition, Chase said that Jedediah Munroe of Lexington was killed in Parker's ambush and that Francis Brown was seriously wounded.[4] The fifty-four year old Munroe was earlier wounded in the dawn skirmish on Lexington Common. Frank Coburn, on the other hand, agrees with Phinney that Parker's men went into action in Lincoln "not far from the Nelson and Hastings homes."[5]

---

[1] Frank Warren Coburn, The Battle of April 19, 1775, Muster Rolls, F. L. Coburn and Co., Boston, 1912, pp. 5-7.

[2] Reverend Ezra Ripley, A History of the Fight at Concord on the 19th of April 1775, Allen and Atwell, Concord, 1927, p. 31.

[3] Elias Phinney, History of the Battle at Lexington, Phelps and Farnham, Boston, 1825, p. 25.

[4] Ellen Chase, The Beginnings of the American Revolution, Volume III, Sir Isaac Pitman and Sons, Ltd., London, 1911, p. 78.

[5] Coburn, p. 104.

Due to the lack of detail and conflicting accounts concerning the location of the Lexington Company when it entered the battle in the afternoon, it is perhaps best to say only that the ambush occurred near the Lincoln-Lexington line. After opening fire on the British, Captain Parker and his men were forced to withdraw by the pressure applied against his force by the flank guard, which was probably reinforced for the occasion.

Parker's casualties in this action could not have been many. Of the ten men killed from Lexington on April 19, 1775, seven were killed on or near Lexington Common in the morning. Benjamin Pierce was also killed in the dawn conflict but he was from Salem. Ten men from Lexington were reported as being wounded on April 19. Ten is also the traditional figure given for the number of Lexington men wounded on or near Lexington Common in the first fighting of the day. It would appear that only three men from Lexington were killed in the afternoon fighting at one point or another.

The British casualties in the action near the Lincoln-Lexington line are not recorded. In their exposed position in the road, the King's Troops must have received some casualties, especially if the Americans deployed along the growth-covered ridge. In removing a boulder from the ridge about 1895, John Lannon, a local farmer, found a sword which had been buried at a depth of about four feet. Apparently, the sword was of British make and of the 1775 period. A lead musket ball, much flattened from its impact with the ledge which pervades the ridge, was also found by Mr. Lannon.[6] The sword could have been buried in a British officer's grave, although there was apparently no remains of the body visible when the sword was found. The ball, of course, could have been fired at Lexington or perhaps Cambridge men in Captain Samuel Thatcher's company concealed on the ridge.

As the British moved further into Lexington, they passed the Whittemore Farmhouse and a structure the Reverend Edmund

---

[6] Ibid., p. 106.

Foster referred to as Benjamin's Tavern.[7] Frank Coburn called this tavern the Bull's Tavern and said that it was called the Viles Tavern in later years. In any case, Coburn repeated the traditional story that the British soldiers ransacked the structure for food and drink and left no money for what they consumed.[8] If the British did indeed take the time to refresh themselves at the tavern, they were probably not under heavy fire at this point. The rear of the British column was probably hard-pressed if not engaged by the colonial forces following them, so this writer suspects that if the tavern was visited, it was done so by soldiers in the more forward elements of the column who were not under much fire, if any.

As the British passed what may have been called Bull's Tavern, they would pass a hill or bluff as it is traditionally called. This bluff was located to the left of the road as it turned northeast. According to the Reverend Foster's account, the British posted a small body of their troops on the north side of the hill. Reverend Foster stated that these troops fired on an unarmed rider who had just rode up. Both the horse and the rider fell to the ground under the British firing. According to the Reverend Foster, the horse was killed but the rider escaped injury.[9]

The Reverend Foster witnessed the death of the horse from apparently a short distance away as he states, "We were quickly at the spot, from which we returned the fire."[10] The British either withdrew from the bluff or were driven off it by the Massachusetts men who were pressing their rear. The Reverend Edmund Foster, of course, was a member of Captain John Brooks' Reading Company which had entered the battle at Meriam's Corner. The British rear was probably under pressure

---

[7] Ripley, p. 34.

[8] Coburn, p. 106.

[9] Ripley, p. 34.

[10] Ibid.

at this point from those companies who had engaged them at Meriam's Corner, Hardy's Hill, and the Bloody Angle area. In addition, companies from Lexington and Cambridge were now in action against the British. It is unclear at this point as to how much of the long British column was under fire. Certainly, the rear was engaged, but the British posted on the bluff must have reduced pressure on the left flank until they withdrew from their elevated position. According to Frank Coburn, two British soldiers are buried "A little way from the bluff, over the wall on the opposite side of the road and in a southerly direction."[11] History does not record how many Americans, if any, were casualties of the fighting near the bluff in Lexington.

Shortly after passing the bluff, the van of the British column would come to the high ground known as Fiske Hill. The best account of the action that occurred here is again given by the Reverend Foster. According to his account:

"The enemy were then rising and passing over Fiske's Hill. An officer, mounted on an elegant horse, and with a drawn sword in his hand, was riding backwards and forwards, commanding and urging on the British troops. A number of Americans behind a pile of rails, raised their guns and fired with deadly effect. The officer fell, and the horse took fright, leaped the wall, and ran directly towards those who had killed his rider. The enemy discharged their musketry in that direction, but their fire took no effect."[12]

Historians generally agree that the officer in question was the Marine Major John Pitcairn who, of course, did not receive his fatal wound until the following June on Breed's Hill in Charlestown. In any event, after the frightened horse was caught, the unseated officer's fine brace of pistols were removed from their holsters by Massachusetts hands. These weapons were later auctioned off in Concord where they were purchased by Captain Nathan Barrett. The Concord militia captain gave them to

[11] Coburn, p. 107.

[12] Ripley, p. 35.

General Israel Putnam, who according to tradition, carried them throughout the war. Later, a descendent of General Putnam gave them to the Town of Lexington.[13] The pistols presently repose in the Hancock-Clarke House in Lexington.

Apparently, the level of fire increased on the flanks as the British reached the Fiske Hill area. It should be noted, however, that historical documentation concerning the specifics of the fighting in this area is far too inadequate to provide the basis of a detailed account. It would appear that a British officer, probably Major Pitcairn, tried to rally his men on Fiske Hill, but as historian Robert Ronsheim pointed out, there is not enough evidence to conclude that the British soldiers were in a full panic and out of control on Fiske Hill or at any point preceding the Fiske Hill area on the road back to Boston. There may have been some confusion in the ranks, however, as evidenced by the mounted officer's attempt to rally the troops in the Fiske Hill area.[14]

According to Historian Frank Coburn, Lt. Col. Francis Smith was shot through the leg on the western slope of Fiske Hill. Coburn cites Ensign John DeBerniere's report to General Gage as evidence for the British officer's wound on Fiske Hill. After reading Ensign DeBerniere's account carefully, however, this writer feels that Lt. Col. Smith could very well have received his leg wound further eastward on the road at Concord Hill.

One account that is related to the Fiske Hill fighting involves an individual encounter between James Hayward of Acton and an unknown British soldier. Apparently, the British soldier had lingered in the Ebenezer Fiske homestead to loot the red structure of what property he could carry off in his pockets. At that time the Ebenezer Fiske house was located near the junction of the Concord Road and present-day Wood Street (referred to

---

[13] Ibid., p. 107.

[14] Robert Ronsheim, "Troop Movement Map: Narrative Section" (unpublished report), Minute Man National Historical Park, 1964, p. 28.

in the 18th century as Clay Road or Cutler Road).[15] According to tradition, Ebenezer Fiske's home stood on the south side of the road the British were following.[16]

According to the traditional Acton account, twenty-five year old James Hayward left his father's house in Acton on the morning of April 19, 1775, with one pound of powder and forty musket balls. As the British retreated from Concord, he followed them and was eager and active in the attack on the King's men. When young Hayward reached Ebenezer Fiske's house on Fiske Hill, he stopped at Fiske's well to quench his thirst. In the meantime, the British soldier who had remained in the house to plunder leveled his musket at Hayward from or near Fiske's doorway. Apparently, Hayward spotted the soldier at about the same time, and they both fired at about the same instant. The British soldier was killed on the spot and the Acton man was mortally wounded. The ball of the British soldier had passed through the lower part of Hayward's powder-horn, driving the splinters into his body. According to the traditional account, James Hayward in the eight hours he lingered repeatedly expressed his willingness to die in defending the rights of his country as he saw them. It was noted at the time that young Hayward had expended nearly all of the powder and balls he had left home with.[17]

James Hayward, according to the traditional story, was not liable for military service, as an earlier injury with an ax had cost him several toes on one foot. He was eager to serve, however, and was among the first to arrive at the home of Captain Isaac Davis on the morning of the 19th. There he was seen at a grindstone putting a point on his bayonet. When asked why he

[15] Joyce Lee Malcolm, The Scene of the Battle, 1775: Historic Grounds Report, Minute Man National Historical Park, Concord, 1983, p. 12.

[16] Josiah Adams, An Address Delivered at Acton, July 21, 1835 Being the First Centennial Anniversary of the Organization of that Town, J. F. Buckingham, Boston, 1835, p. 48.

[17] Ibid.

did it, he was said to reply, "I expect before the night, we shall come to a push with them and I want my bayonet sharp."[18]

James Hayward was apparently well-educated for his day as he had once taught school. He was also a man who strongly believed in the patriot cause, as his physical handicap would have excused him from military service. Hayward, however, wished only to serve and in that respect he was a volunteer in the highest sense.

The Haywood encounter at the well with the unknown British soldier is a good story and needs no embellishment to make it interesting. Historians, however, have expanded the story to include a dialogue between the luckless opponents. According to the inscription on the tablet presently located near an old well in the yard of Ebenezer Fiske:

"At this well
April 19, 1775
James Hayward of Acton
met a British soldier
who raising his gun said
'You are a dead man.'
'And so are you,' replied Hayward.
Both fired. The soldier
was instantly killed
& Hayward mortally wounded."

According to Ellen Chase, some pieces of jewelry the soldier had pilfered from the Fiske House dropped into the pigs' trough, which when later recovered, showed traces of pigs' teeth.[19] Apparently, the ill-fated soldier was not the only plunderer of the Fiske House, as only some of the missing items were found on his body. Items apparently carried away by other soldiers

---

[18] D. Hamilton Hurd, <u>History of Middlesex County, Massachusetts</u>, J. W. Lewis Co., Philadelphia, 1880, p. 257.

[19] Chase, Vol. III, p. 77.

included: four fine Holland shirts, a black silk apron, a gold ring, one stone earring, a pair of stone sleeve buttons, one black gauze handkerchief, one black Barcelona handkerchief, two pair cotton hose, six shillings, and a one-quart pewter baron. In addition, one sash window was apparently smashed by the British soldiers.[20]

The fact that the British looted Ebenezer Fiske's home and the items that were missing after they left is based on solid documentation. The looters probably felt that their lives were in no immediate danger or they would not have taken the time to search for the small items that they carried off. Therefore, this writer agrees with Historian Ronsheim that the evidence for intense fighting or British panic on Fiske Hill is weak. Men died on Fiske Hill or near to it, but the breakdown of discipline which resulted in the panic, or near panic, of the King's troops more likely occurred on Concord Hill rather than Fiske Hill.

As the British left the Fiske Hill area, they soon found themselves going up another hill in Lexington, Concord Hill. According to Frank Coburn, the summit of Concord Hill is some 40 feet higher than Fiske Hill and at least 80 feet higher than Lexington Common.[21] Concord Hill is within a mile to the westward of Lexington Common. The British soldiers, and especially the flankers, were very tired at this point, as they had marched over 23 miles without the benefit of a night's rest. Moreover, it would appear that they were actually surrounded on Concord Hill by what must have appeared to them a moving circle of armed Americans. The account of Reverend Foster states that after the British passed Thaddeus Reed's house, which was located on the western slope of Concord Hill, the British came under fire from all directions.[22]

---

[20] Massachusetts State Archives, Vol. 138, p. 407.

[21] Coburn, p. 110.

[22] Ripley, p. 35.

The account of the British Lieutenant John Barker also indicates that the British were surrounded. According to Barker's account:

"In this way we marched between 9 and 10 miles, their numbers increasing from all parts, while ours was reducing by deaths, wounds and fatigue, and we were totally surrounded with such an incessant fire as it's impossible to conceive, our ammunition was likewise near expended. In this critical situation, we perceived the 1st Brigade coming to our assistance."[23]

From the summit or western slope of Concord Hill the British would have been in a position to see Lord Hugh Earl Percy's brigade as it approached east of Lexington Common. As Lt. Barker indicated, the British troops were in a "critical situation" when they sighted Percy's brigade. This is good evidence, therefore, that the most critical point of the British return to Boston occurred on Concord Hill and not Fiske Hill where they would not have been able to see Percy's brigade.

Perhaps the best account of the situation along this stretch of the road is contained in the account of Ensign John DeBerniere:

"Within a mile of Lexington, our ammunition began to fail, and the light companies were so fatigued with flanking they were scarce able to act, and a great number of wounded scarce able to get forward, made a great confusion; Col. Smith (our commanding officer) had received a wound through his leg, a number of officers were also wounded, so that we began to run rather than retreat in order...the whole behaved with amazing bravery, but little order; we attempted to stop the men and form them two deep, but to no purpose, the confusion increased rather than lessened: At last after we got through Lexington, the officers got to the front and presented their bayonets, and told the men if they advanced they should die: Upon this they began to form under a very heavy fire; but at that instant, the first brigade joined us,

[23] Elizabeth Ellery Dana, Editor, The British in Boston, Being the Diary of Lt. John Barker of the King's Own Regiment from November 15, 1774 to May 31, 1776, Harvard University Press, Cambridge, 1924, p. 35.

consisting of the 4th, 23d, and 47th regiments, and two divisions of marines, under the command of Brigadier-General Lord Percy."[24]

Ensign DeBerniere probably considered Lexington Common as Lexington, so the reader should view his remarks "within a mile of Lexington" and "through Lexington" in this light. Concord Hill, of course, is within a mile of Lexington Common, and it is entirely likely that Lt. Col. Smith and his officers would try to form their confused ranks into some kind of military order, especially under the gaze of Lord Percy and his brigade. This attempt to reorganize the disorderly and exhausted troops probably occurred east of Lexington Common as Percy approached and deployed his force. Perhaps Smith hoped the colonials would assemble into a formation on Lexington Common where he and Percy's force could either make a stand or counterattack the Provincials. In any event, Percy would open his ranks long enough to allow the exhausted men under Smith's command to pass through where they could enjoy a temporary rest behind the protective red wall of the First Brigade.

It is not hard to imagine the great joy and relief Smith and his men must have experienced upon the sight of Lord Percy's First Brigade as it deployed on the high ground east of Lexington Common. Greatly fatigued, low on ammunition, their ranks reduced by deaths and serious wounds, the spirits of the hard-pressed British soldiers must have vastly improved at the sight of Percy's brigade of about 1,000 men as it deployed in a linear defensive formation on the rising ground just east of Lexington Common.

For a considerable time before he sighted Smith's force, Lord Hugh Earl Percy had heard the sound of heavy firing as the desperate British passed over Concord Hill. Upon reaching the high ground east of the Common, Percy quickly ordered his force to deploy and his artillery men to make ready to fire the

---

[24] Vincent J.R. Kehoe, We Were There! April 19, 1775, The British Soldiers, "Ensign DeBerniere's Account," Chelmsford, Massachusetts, 1974, p. 122.

two field pieces they had brought with them. In his official report to General Gage, Percy described the situation as follows:

"His Majesty's Troops, who were retiring, overpowered by numbers, greatly exhausted and fatigued, having expended almost all their ammunition. And about two o'clock I met them retiring through the Town of Lexington.

I immediately ordered the 2-field pieces to fire at the Rebels, and drew up the Brigade on a height. The shot from the cannon had the desired effect, and stopped the Rebels for a little time, who immediately dispersed, and endeavoured to surround us, being very numerous."[25]

The colonials were not accustomed to being subject to cannon fire and the balls fired at them discouraged them from forming into any kind of mass formation to attack the British. This is probably fortunate for the Provincials, as their encirclement tactics were working well and there is no evidence that a massed attack on the reinforced British force would have been successful at this location.

In any case, the success or failure of British arms was no longer the responsibility of Lt. Col. Francis Smith. The old soldier had carried out his orders in a difficult situation to the best of his limited ability and now the fate of British lives were in the highly capable hands of Acting Brigadier General Hugh Percy, the Earl of Northumberland.

---

[25] Charles Knowles Bolton, Editor, Letters of Hugh Earl Percy, Boston and New York, 1774-76, Charles E. Goodspeed, Boston, 1902, p. 50.

7 – PERCY'S MARCH TO LEXINGTON

In command of the First Brigade, General Thomas Gage had placed thirty-two year old Acting Brigadier General Hugh Earl Percy. Hugh Percy was the son of Sir Hugh Smithson and Lady Elizabeth Seymour, daughter of the Earl of Northumberland. Lady Elizabeth was also the heiress of the Percy barony and great family estates of the ancient and respected House of Percy.[1]

In 1750 upon succeeding his father-in-law as Earl of Northumberland, Sir Hugh Smithson took the name of Percy. In 1776, he was created Earl Percy and Duke of Northumberland. The Duke's eldest son, Hugh, used the title Earl Percy during his military service in America.[2]

The Duke of Northumberland had voted against the Stamp Act and in other ways had shown disapproval of the British Government's policy toward America. His son Hugh was also supportive of the Duke's views on colonial policy. Hugh was a

---

[1] Charles Knowles Bolton, Editor, <u>Letters of Hugh Earl Percy from Boston and New York 1774 - 1776</u>, Charles E. Goodspeed, Boston, 1902, p. 15.

[2] Ibid., pp. 15-16.

loyal soldier, however, and when ordered to America in 1774, he left his native England to serve with his regiment in Boston.[3]

Lord Percy was well liked by the men of his regiment. When his regiment was ordered to America, Percy spent 700 pounds of his own money in hiring transports to carry over the soldiers' wives and children. He also fitted out these dependents with necessary items for the voyage.[4]

Percy also enjoyed some support at home where in the fall of 1774, after he had arrived in America, the voters of Westminster re-elected him to his seat in Parliament. During the course of a bitter election, Percy's campaign workers were encouraged by the support given to their absent candidate by Lord North, the Prime Minister.[5]

Despite Earl Percy's earlier sympathy with the American arguments against British colonial policy, he had no sympathy for rebellion and believed that Britain must take a hard line in order to restore orderly government in Massachusetts. In a letter to his father dated from Boston on July 27, 1774, Percy wrote in part:

"Till you make their Committees of Correspondence and Congress with the other colonies high treason, and try them for it in England, you must never expect perfect obedience and submission from this to the Mother Country."[6]

In his early days in America, Lord Percy also held a low opinion of the colonials he met and observed in the Boston area. In the same letter to his father, the Duke of Northumberland, he wrote:

---

[3] Ibid., p. 16.

[4] Ibid., p. 18.

[5] Ibid., p. 20.

[6] Ibid., p. 29.

"The people in this part of the country are in general made up of rashness and timidity. Quick and violent in their determinations, they are fearful in the execution of them (unless, indeed, they are quite certain of meeting little or no opposition, and then, like all other cowards, they are cruel and tyrannical). To hear them talk, you would imagine that they would attack us and demolish us every night; and yet, whenever we appear, they are frightened out of their wits."[7]

By September 12, 1774, Lord Percy considered Massachusetts to be in open rebellion. As he remarked to his father in a letter of that date, "In short, this country is now in as open a state of rebellion as Scotland was in the year [17]45."[8] Percy recognized the danger the existing militia laws presented to Gage's army when he wrote in the same letter:

"What makes an insurrection here always more formidable than in other places, is that there is a law of this Province, which obliges every inhabitant to be furnished with a firelock, bayonet, and pretty considerable quantity of ammunition. Besides which, every township is obliged by the same law to have a large magazine of all kinds of military stores."[9]

As Lord Percy watched the military preparations the Massachusetts militia was making in the fall of 1774, he became convinced that military action would be required in order to restore orderly British rule. In a letter to the Rev. Thomas Percy dated November 25, 1774, Percy wrote:

"In short they have now got to such lengths that nothing can secure the colonies to the Mother Country, but the Conquest of them. The people here

---

[7] Ibid., pp. 28-29.

[8] Ibid., p. 37.

[9] Ibid., p. 38.

are the most designing, artful villains in the world. They have not the least idea of either religion or morality."[10]

In the person of Acting Brigadier General Hugh Earl Percy, the people of Massachusetts faced a dangerous and highly capable professional soldier fully dedicated to their subjection to the laws and rule of the British King. Percy, moreover, held the Provincials in low regard and was supremely confident of the moral superiority of the British cause and the ultimate victory of British arms.

Shortly after his arrival in Boston in the summer of 1774, General Thomas Gage had appointed Colonels Hugh Percy and Robert Pigot as Acting Brigadier Generals. This was their American rank, as Percy was normally the Colonel of the 5th Regiment of Foot. Pigot's rank in the permanent army establishment was also Colonel, although he served as Lt. Col. of the 38th Regiment of Foot. On April 19, 1775, Gage's army in Boston was brigaded into the 1st, 2nd, and 3rd Brigades under the commands of Acting Brigadier Generals Percy, Pigot, and Valentine Jones, respectively.[11]

The 1st Brigade Lord Percy commanded on April 19, 1775 consisted of the 4th Regiment of Foot (King's Own), the 23rd Regiment of Foot (Royal Welch Fusiliers), the 47th Regiment of Foot, and the 1st Battalion of Marines. The grenadiers and light infantry companies had been detached to the command of Lt. Col. Francis Smith for his Concord expedition, so Percy's regiments on the morning of April 19 contained only eight companies in each instead of the usual ten companies a British regiment was normally assigned at that time.

General Gage probably realized that the departure of Lt. Col. Smith's detachment to Concord was no surprise to the Boston populace. Before Gage retired for the night, feeling that Smith

---

[10] Ibid., p. 44.

[11] Vincent J. R. Kehoe, We Were There! April 19, 1775: The British Soldiers, Chelmsford, Massachusetts, 1974, p. 12.

might need help, he ordered Percy's 1st Brigade to parade at 4 a.m. on April 19. Gage's orders were carried to the quarters of the Brigade Major Captain Thomas Moncrieffe. As Moncrieffe was absent from his home, the orders were left with his servant. The Brigade Major came home late and apparently went to bed. The servant forgot to tell Captain Moncrieffe of the orders on the table. Thus at 4 a.m., the 1st Brigade still slumbered in their beds.[12]

About 5 a.m. or so the express Smith had sent back arrived and requested reinforcements. By at least 6 o'clock, orders directed to the various regiments cleared 1st Brigade Headquarters. The foul-up in orders at the Brigade Major's House had been costly, however, as the 23rd Regiment of Foot, for example, did not receive its order to assemble until 7 a.m. This order called for the regiment to assemble on the "Grand Parade" at 7:30 a.m.[13]

At the designated hour of 7:30 a.m. the 4th, 23rd, and 47th regiments were on parade as ordered. The Brigade was further delayed, however, as the Marines did not receive the order until the other regiments of the Brigade had assembled. Finally, at about 8:30 a.m. the Marines arrived. It seems that the order to assemble the Marines had been addressed to Major John Pitcairn and left at his quarters. Pitcairn, of course, was in no position to take action on the order as he had gone to Concord with Smith's detachment.[14]

The two foul-ups in orders had delayed the departure of Percy's Brigade for almost five hours. These mistakes in orders hurt the British badly, as Gage intended Percy to march at 4 a.m. or shortly thereafter. Had Percy marched earlier, he could have

---

[12] Allen French, The Day of Concord and Lexington, Little Brown, Boston, 1925, p. 226.

[13] Allen French, Editor, A British Fusilier in Revolutionary Boston, "Diary of Lt. Frederick Mackenzie," Cambridge, Harvard University Press, 1926, pp. 52-53.

[14] Ibid.

reinforced Smith in Concord and led the return march from its onset.

As the three regiments stood waiting for the Marines to join them, they were observed about 7 a.m. by Harrison Gray Otis, who was then nine years old. Otis recalled in later years:

"On the 19th of April, 1775, I went to school for the last time. In the morning about seven, Percy's Brigade was drawn up, extending from Scollay's buildings, through Tremont St., and nearly to the bottom of the Mall, preparing to take up the march for Lexington."[15]

According to Lt. Frederick Mackenzie, the Adjutant of the Royal Welch Fusiliers, Lord Percy's 1st Brigade marched at 8:45 a.m. in the following order: Advanced guard of a Captain and 50 men, two six-pound artillery pieces, the 4th Regiment, the 47th Regiment, the 1st Battalion of Marines, the 23rd Regiment, and the rear guard of a Captain and 50 men.[16]

Percy's brigade marched out of Boston over the Neck, through Roxbury and across the "Great Bridge" into Cambridge. It is said that during this stretch of the march, Percy's fife and drummers struck up the tune "Yankee Doodle" in defiance of the watching colonials. Later London wits of the day and others would link Lord Percy's march to the Chevy Chase ballad:

"To drive the deer with hound and Home
Erle Percy took his way.
the child may rue that is unborne
the hunting of that day!"[17]

In any event, at the bridge spanning the Charles River, the advance guard found that the Provincials had removed the

---

[15] French, pp. 227-228.

[16] French, "Mackenzie's Diary," p. 53.

[17] French, pp. 228-229.

planks. Soldiers were able to cross the bridge on stringers, however, and finding the planks neatly piled on the Cambridge side, they replaced enough of them so the Brigade could cross. According to tradition, Percy left the men of his supply train to complete the plank-laying process and continued his march leaving the supply train behind.[18]

It is hard to believe that an officer of Percy's experience would leave his supply train behind without adequate protection. The fact is, however, that the small supply train did lag behind Percy's Brigade and was captured by colonial irregulars in the Town of Menotomy (present day Arlington).

Percy's supply train probably consisted of only a wagon or two. It was placed under the guard of a sergeant and 11 men. In the meantime, news of the approach of the wagon train had reached Menotomy. According to the traditional story, about a dozen elderly men including David Lamson, Jason Belknap, Joe Belknap, James Budge, Israel Mead, and Ammi Cutter gathered under arms. Apparently, they elected Lamson, a man of mixed blood who has been described in the traditional stories as both a mulatto or half-Indian, as their leader. The Rev. Phillips Payson of Chelsea also participated in this affair.[19]

Lamson's small force of aging belligerents deployed in an ambush position behind a stone wall on the northerly side of the road, almost opposite the First Parish Meeting House. According to the traditional story, Lamson shouted at the sergeant to surrender, but a driver whipped his horses in an attempt to escape the trap. The elderly patriots opened fire, killing two soldiers, wounding several others, and also killing several horses. The surviving soldiers ran for their lives, allowing the wagon train to fall into the hands of the Menotomy men.[20]

---

[18] Ibid., pp. 229-230.

[19] Frank W. Coburn, The Battle of April 19, 1775, F. L. Coburn, Co., Boston, 1912, p. 119.

[20] Ibid.

According to the traditional story, some soldiers who fled the supply train ran southerly along the western shore of Spy Pond, as far as Spring Valley, where they came upon an old lady picking dandelions. This elderly Menotomy woman was known as Mother Batherick. The soldiers surrendered themselves to the elderly lady who led them to the home of Captain Ephraim Frost. The British were unarmed at this time, as previous to meeting Mother Batherick some of them had thrown their muskets in Spy Pond. Another man had bent his musket by banging it on purpose over a stone wall. According to the tradition, as Mother Batherick turned the British Regulars over to a party of Provincials at Captain Frost's house she said to the Britons: "If you ever live to get back, you tell King George that an old woman took six of his grenadiers prisoners."[21]

The picture the British soldiers conveyed by throwing away their arms and surrendering to an old unarmed woman is hardly the image one associates with a highly motivated, elite professional fighting force. Indeed, it is simply the image of frightened men, in fear for their lives, motivated mainly by a strong will to survive, and finding their key to survival behind the protection of a woman's skirts. When the news of this incident reached the opposition press in England, it was printed that, "If an old Yankee woman can take six grenadiers, how many soldiers will it require to conquer America?"[22]

Lord Percy, as he rode along with his brigade, which must have contained about a thousand officers and men, was unaware at first of the determined opposition Lt. Col. Francis Smith had met with on his return march from Concord. In his diary, Lt. Frederick Mackenzie remarked:

"We went out of Boston by the neck, and marched through Roxbury, Cambridge and Monotomy, towards Lexington. In all the places we marched

[21] Ellen Chase, The Beginnings of the American Revolution, Vol. III, Sir Isaac Pitman and Sons, Ltd., London, 1911, p. 108.

[22] Ibid., pp. 108-109.

through, and in the houses on the road, few or no people were to be seen; and the houses were in general shut up."[23]

In Menotomy, a person who Percy met first informed him that Lt. Col. Smith's detachment had been engaged by the Provincials. The British leader learned even more details when he met the wounded Lt. Edward Gould of the 4th (King's Own) Regiment on his way back in a chaise. Of these encounters, Percy wrote in his official report to General Gage:

"At Menotomy, I was informed by a person whom I met that there had been a skirmish between his Majestie's troops and the rebels at Lexington, and that they were still engaged. On this, I immediately pressed on, in less than two miles we heard the firing very distinctly. About this time (which was between 1 and 2 o'clock in the afternoon) I met with Lt. Gould of the King's Own Reg., who was wounded, and who informed me that the Gren. and L.I. had been attacked by the rebels about daybreak, and were retiring, having expended most of their ammunition."[24]

As the reader will recall, Lt. Edward Thoroton Gould was one of four British officers wounded earlier in the day at Concord's North Bridge. Gould, suffering from a foot wound, left Percy and continued down the road in his commandeered chaise. His journey would end, however, in Menotomy village, as he was captured by some of the old men who had taken part in the capture of Percy's supply train.[25] As a prisoner, he was taken to Medford, where he signed an affidavit on April 25, 1775. His signed statement said, in part, that the British fired first at Concord's North Bridge. Gould's affidavit was later printed in the English press. Gould eventually returned to England following his exchange, but his days in the army were numbered.

---

[23] French, "Mackenzie's Diary," p. 53.

[24] Bolton, "Percy's Official Report to Gage," p. 51.

[25] Coburn, p. 121.

On January 26, 1776 he sold out his commission and left military service.[26]

According to Lt. Mackenzie's diary entry, Percy's brigade first heard the shots coming from about a mile down the road in front of them. At first, the noise of the shooting appeared to Mackenzie to be that of straggling fire, but as the gap between Percy's column and Smith's closed, the noise of the shooting became plainer with greater frequency. Mackenzie described the situation in the following words:

At half after 2, being near the church at Lexington, and the fire encreasing, we were ordered to form the Line, which was immediately done by extending on each side of the road, but by reason of the stone walls and other obstructions, it was not formed in so regular a manner as it should have been. The Grenadiers and Light Infantry were at this time retiring towards Lexington, fired upon by the Rebels, who took every advantage the face of the country afforded them. As soon as the Grenadiers and Light Infantry perceived the 1st Brigade drawn up for their support, they shouted repeatedly, and the firing ceased for a short time.[27]

It must have been an emotionally charged moment for the hard-pressed Regulars in Smith's column when they first caught sight of Lord Percy's brigade. Smith's force had passed by Lexington Common on their left and were about a half mile beyond the Common on the road toward Boston when they joined with Percy. The Brigadier General opened his ranks and Smith's desperate, exhausted troops passed through where most of them, almost totally spent, sank to the ground for much needed rest.

Percy, the archetype of the cool British commander, had quickly sized up the situation and had deployed his line on an elevation, where his troops could command the road and the approach from the Lexington Common area. Percy saw that the

---

[26] Kehoe, p. 109.

[27] French, "Mackenzie's Diary," p. 54.

Provincials were much scattered, but that a group of them seemed to be clustered in the road near the Meeting House on Lexington Common. Percy quickly ordered his two six-pound field pieces into action and dispersed the groups by firing cannon balls in their direction.[28]

The cannon balls Percy's gunners fired at the Americans did not kill anyone, but the Meeting House was hit and damaged. As noted earlier, the Provincials were not accustomed to standing firm under cannon fire, which would bowl over troops in a massed formation like tenpins in a bowling alley. By scattering at the sound of the cannon, the Massachusetts men did not provide Percy's gunners with a large target to shoot at. On the other hand, Percy attained his objective, which was to check the colonials from forming into any type of mass formation from which they could launch a direct assault upon his line. It can be said of Percy, that his two six-pound field pieces fired the first cannon shots by the British Army at American militia troops of the Revolutionary War.

Percy knew that delay in Lexington would give even more Provincials the opportunity to make contact with his force, but he had to give Smith's exhausted men a chance to regain their strength. He also had to see that the wounded in Smith's ranks were provided for before he could start his march back to Boston.

As Smith's flank companies rested behind the 1st Brigade's line, the Provincials who were closest to the British opened fire. The British returned this fire, but it was not effective as the Americans, for the most part, were concealed behind stone walls and trees. Other colonials crept into the covered ground on either side of the British line in an attempt to flank Percy's force. The British advanced some of their best marksmen, who fired at any American who showed himself. At that time there was what Lt. Mackenzie described as a morass in front of his regiment's

---

[28] Bolton, "Percy's Official Report to Gage," p. 50.

left, which probably kept many of the Provincials from getting within effective musket range.[29]

Percy had deployed his two cannon in separate locations on hills on either side of the road to Boston. One cannon, the nearest to the Common, was placed on an elevation to the right side of the road in the triangle area between the roads to Boston and Woburn. The other cannon was placed on an elevation on the left side of the road to the rear of the more advanced cannon. This latter cannon was on the same side of the road as the Munroe Tavern on the Lexington Common side of the Tavern.

Percy's line faced the village of Lexington and Lexington Common. Vine Brook flowed between the British line and the bulk of the Americans. A morass on Percy's left front also helped to keep the opposing sides apart. His troops, deployed across the road and high ground and supported by cannon, were in a good defensive position.

Munroe Tavern, which was situated beside the road about a quarter of a mile behind the British line, was utilized by Percy as a temporary shelter for the wounded and headquarters and place of refreshment for the British officers. The owner of the tavern, William Munroe, was a sergeant on duty with Captain John Parker's Lexington Militia Company. In his absence, Munroe had left a lame man, John Raymond, in charge of the tavern. The British kept Raymond busy with their demands for liquor and service. The lame man must have found this service very tiring and doubtless distasteful. Perhaps something that he overheard made him fearful for his life. In any event he tried to flee, but was shot down in the yard.[30] The death of the non-combatant Raymond, appears to have been one of those senseless tragedies often associated with war. Before leaving the tavern, the British tried to burn it down, but the flames were extinguished after they left.

---

[29] French, "Mackenzie's Diary," p. 55.

[30] Coburn, p. 127.

While the British under Percy were in Lexington, a number of private buildings were burned and looted, while others were simply looted. The buildings that were burned were mainly alongside the road in the area of Percy's line. The houses that were burned were done so in the vicinity of Percy's line and probably he had given orders for their destruction in order to prevent colonial snipers from firing upon his rear guard when he would begin his march to Boston. The British soldiers, apparently under orders from their officers, pushed over about 200 rods of stone walls belonging to Deacon Joseph Loring. Historian Frank Coburn attributes this act to strong British hostility toward the Americans, but the walls were more likely pushed over to prevent the colonials from firing on the troops from positions behind them. The British also destroyed Deacon Loring's home, barn, and corn house by fire. The home of Lydia Mulliken and the nearby clock shop of Nathaniel Mulliken were burned as well as the home and shop of Joshua Bond. According to the affidavit of Elijah Sanderson, the British set fire to several other buildings, but the flames were extinguished after the British departed.[31]

The British also looted a number of homes in the vicinity of Percy's line, but did not burn them. They were probably looking for concealed militia men in these structures, and once inside the homes, they couldn't resist the opportunity to carry off small portable items. The home of Matthew Mead, which stood on the easterly side of the road, nearly opposite the Loring residence, was one of several homes in Lexington that were looted but not burned.[32]

Frank Coburn was highly critical of Earl Percy for destroying the three private homes and several shops in Lexington. It would appear, however, that Percy only burned those structures that were potential shelters for colonial snipers. His motives then

---

[31] Elias Phinney, <u>History of the Battle at Lexington</u>, "Affidavit of Elias Sanderson, Dec. 17, 1824," Phelps and Farnham, Boston, 1825, p. 33.

[32] Coburn, p. 124.

were primarily tactical and by destroying the homes he may have saved some British lives. History does not record, however, that Percy took any steps to prevent his soldiers from looting the Lexington houses. Doubtless his mind was absorbed with many details relating to his withdrawal from Lexington, and the actions of his soldiers in regard to looting at this point may have gone unnoticed by him.

Earl Percy doubtless realized that time was not in his favor. The longer he stayed in Lexington, the more time his colonial opponents would have to reach a point along the road to Boston where they could harass the King's troops. Shortly after 3 p.m., the Royal Welch Fusiliers received Percy's order to form the rear guard. Acting Brigadier General Hugh Earl Percy was about to lead his men along the difficult road to Boston. It would be a march that Percy and the men who survived it would long remember.

8 – PERCY'S RETURN FROM LEXINGTON THROUGH MENOTOMY

Acting Brigadier General Hugh Earl Percy knew that time was not on his side. He had to start his march back to Boston soon, before the strength of the colonials became too great. He, therefore, issued orders to the 23rd Regiment (Royal Welch Fusiliers) to form the rear guard. The Adjutant of the 23rd Regiment, Lt. Frederick Mackenzie, provided the following account of Percy's initial marching disposition as follows:

"At about 1/4 past 3, Earl Percy having come to a resolution of returning to Boston, and having made his disposition for that purpose, our Regiment received orders to form the rear guard. We immediately lined the walls and other cover with some marksmen, and retired from the right of companies by files to the high ground a small distance in our rear, where we again formed in line, and remained in that position for near half an hour, during which time the flank companies, and the other Regiments of the Brigade, began their march in one column on the road towards Cambridge."[1]

---

[1] Allen French, Ed., <u>A British Fusilier in Revolutionary Boston</u>, "Mackenzie's Diary," Harvard University Press, Cambridge, 1926, p. 55.

In his official report to General Thomas Gage, Lord Percy remarked concerning his initial marching formation from Lexington:

"As it began now to grow pretty late, & we had 15 miles to retire, & only our 36 rounds, I ordered the Grenadiers and Lgt Infy to move off first, & covered them with my Brigade, sending out very strong flanking parties, which were absolutely necessary, as there was not a stone-wall, or house, though before in appearance evacuated, from whence the Rebels did not fire upon us."[2]

Percy's decision to place the tired grenadiers and light infantry of Lt. Francis Smith's detachment in the van of the column was doubtless based on Percy's belief that the forward part of the column would make the least contact with the Provincials. Percy believed that the most dangerous threat to his force would come to the rear guard and he wanted fresh men in that critical position. The men of the 23rd Regiment were fresh and Percy would leave them in the rear guard for the first seven miles of his march from Lexington before he would relieve them with the marines, who marched just ahead of the Royal Welch Fusiliers in the column.[3]

According to Percy, as soon as the Americans saw his troops begin their march, they pressed very close upon his rear guard. Mackenzie wrote that before the column had marched a mile on the road they were fired upon from "all quarters, but particularly from the houses on the roadside, and the adjacent stone walls."[4] Mackenzie went on to write that several soldiers were killed or wounded in this manner.

[2] Charles Knowles Bolton, Ed., Letters of Hugh Earl Percy from Boston and New York 1774-1776, "Percy's Official Account to Gage, April 20, 1775," Charles E. Goodspeed, Boston, 1902, p. 50.

[3] French, "Mackenzie's Diary," p. 56.

[4] Ibid.

According to Frank Coburn, the British crossed the Lexington-Menotomy line about 4:30 on that fateful Wednesday afternoon. The line was about two and one quarter miles from the point in Lexington where Percy began his return march. In Menotomy, the most intense fighting of the day would occur as minute and militia companies from Essex and Norfolk counties would join the Middlesex men in attacking the hard-pressed British column.

It should be noted that the American forces following and harassing the British column now included a high ranking American militia officer, General William Heath, and the famed patriot activist, Dr. Joseph Warren (later Major-General Warren). General Heath had been awakened at daybreak on the 19th and told that the British had crossed the Charles River with Concord as their probable destination. After conferring with the Committee of Safety, General Heath rode to Watertown where he ordered the militia he found there to take up the planks on the bridge spanning the Charles in Cambridge and to take up a position by the bridge. Thus, the British return route to Boston had been impeded by the implementation of General Heath's wise order.[5]

After leaving Watertown, General Heath was joined by Dr. Joseph Warren and the two patriots proceeded to Lexington by a cross road. They arrived in Lexington shortly after Lord Percy had linked up with Lt. Col. Smith's hard-pressed column. Shortly after he arrived on the scene in Lexington, General Heath assisted in reforming an American regiment, which had been disorganized by Percy's cannon shot.[6] It should be noted that without an adequate staff it would be difficult for General Heath to exercise strict command and control over the various regiments and partial regiments that would encounter the British on the road to Charlestown.

---

[5] William Heath, Memoirs of Major-General William Heath by Himself, William Abbatt, New York, 1901, p. 7.

[6] Ibid., pp. 7-8.

According to Frank Coburn, who made an intensive study of the numbers of minute and militia forces involved in the April 19 engagement, the British were pursued by almost 2,000 Americans as they crossed the Lexington line into Menotomy. Coburn's figure included the three companies from Newton under Captains Phineas Cook, Amariah Fuller, and Jeremiah Wiswell. According to the muster rolls, the Newton companies entered the contest at Lexington with a total strength of about 219 men.[7]

The British crossed the Menotomy-Lexington line about 4:30 p.m. In Menotomy the road soon descended Pierce's Hill to level ground in an area now known as Foot of the Rocks. It was near Foot of the Rocks that a musket ball knocked the pin out of the hair of Dr. Warren's earlock.[8] Luck was with Warren this day, however, as he would not receive his fatal wound until the following June at the battle known as Bunker Hill.

There were a number of individual contests between Americans and British soldiers on this fateful Wednesday. One of these life and death struggles, a bayonet duel, occurred between Doctor Eliphalet Downer of Roxbury and an unknown British soldier. This individual confrontation took place not far from the Foot of the Rocks. According to the Downer family tradition, the Roxbury doctor reversed his musket and stunned his British opponent with a swift butt stroke. The Britain dropped to the ground where the good doctor terminated his existence with a deadly bayonet thrust.[9]

As the British column advanced through Menotomy, the Light Infantry flankers entered and searched many of the houses alongside the road. They also carried off many items of value. At the Robbins home, near the summit of Pierce's Hill, the family had fled, but the British ransacked the home and tried to burn it

[7] Frank Warren Coburn, The Battle of April 19, 1775 (Muster Rolls), published by author, Lexington, 1912, pp. 42-44.

[8] Heath, p. 8.

[9] Ibid.

down. After they left, a line full of wet clothes fell into the fire the flankers had set in the kitchen. Fortunately, the wet garments smothered the flames and the Robbins home was spared from destruction.[10]

The Tuft's Tavern, which was a little further down the road from the Robbins home, was also looted, vandalized, and burned by the British flankers, who even left the taps on the casks of molasses and spirits open as they departed. Fortunately, a faithful slave of a Mr. Cutler entered the tavern room after the British left and put out the fire.[11]

The degree to which the consumption of alcohol impaired the judgment of the British soldiers is difficult to judge in an age where the consumption of spirits was heavy among both soldiers and civilians. At least some of the British soldiers, however, especially the flankers, must have been influenced by alcohol as they seem to have refreshed themselves at every tavern they entered along the road.

The British also plundered and burned the home of Deacon Joseph Adams. In addition, they frightened his wife and drove her from bed with her infant child. It seems that Deacon Adams had fled from his home upon the sight of the approaching British. When the British reached his home, some of them, probably flankers, broke open his front door and eventually three of them entered the bed chamber where Mrs. Adams lay with her infant, only a few days old. According to tradition, one of the soldiers opened her bed-curtains and pointed his fixed bayonet to her breast. Mrs. Adams requested that her life be spared, but the soldier is said to have replied: "Damn you!"[12] Fortunately, another soldier interceded and according to tradition he said,

---

[10] Coburn, p. 136.

[11] Ibid., pp. 136-137.

[12] Ibid., p. 138.

"We will not kill the woman if she will go out of the house, but we will surely burn it."[13]

As Mrs. Adams carried her infant to the nearby cornhouse, the British soldiers put their loot in the sheets they had stripped from the beds. Among the items stolen were the works of an old family clock and a silver tankard, which belonged to the Second Precinct Church. Before the British left the home of Deacon Adams, they emptied a basket of wood chips on the floor and set them on fire with a brand from the hearth. According to the tradition, several Adams children who had remained in the house extinguished the fire after the British had left by pouring beer on it.[14]

In the meantime, Deacon Adams had been seen by the soldiers as he fled across the fields to the barn of the Reverend Cook. They fired some shots at the Deacon but he reached the barn unharmed and hid under the hay. The British followed him into the barn and thrust their bayonets into the hay. Fortunately for Deacon Adams, the bayonets failed to make contact and he emerged from the hay after the British left the barn.[15]

A little ways beyond the Adams residence the home of Jason Russell was located on the western side of the road. Russell, a lame man in his late fifties, had remained to watch over his property. He barricaded his gate with bundles of shingles and decided to take up a firing position from behind this impromptu barricade. His neighbor, Ammi Cutler, recognized that Russell was in danger in that poor defensive position, but Russell would not budge. He remarked simply that "An Englishman's house is his castle."[16]

In the meantime, about three hundred men from the nine Danvers' companies of the First Essex Regiment of Militia had

---

[13] Ibid.

[14] Ibid.

[15] Ibid.

[16] Ibid., p. 139.

arrived or were near the Town of Menotomy after a hard 16-mile march from Danvers. Upon hearing the news of the alarm about 8 a.m., Captain Samuel Epes of Danvers rode to Salem to obtain permission to march from the commander of the First Essex Regiment, Colonel Timothy Pickering of Salem. Captain Epes found Colonel Pickering, who had been elected Colonel by a meeting of Captains in February, at work in the Registry of Deeds. Colonel Pickering gave verbal orders to Captain Epes to march at once. Pickering then had a short consultation with the Selectmen of Salem and other leading gentlemen, who agreed that Pickering should march with the rest of his regiment, including the large contingent from Salem, as soon as he could assemble them.[17]

While Colonel Pickering was raising the rest of his regiment, Captain Epes sped back to Danvers with permission to march as soon as the Danvers men were ready. They were ready to march about 10 a.m. Some of the men and officers from Danvers were mounted, and it is quite possible that the mounted men arrived in Menotomy before the men on foot. In any event, the various Danvers companies took several different routes to the scene of action, and it is very unlikely that they arrived at the same time in a single cohesive unit. Five companies from Lynn and three companies from Beverly also entered the Battle at Menotomy and at least some of these companies were near the Danvers companies at the time Danvers went into action. It should be mentioned that a good number of Beverly men marched with Danvers. About half the men in Captain Israel Hutchinson's 53-man Danvers Minute Company were from Beverly according to Coburn's rolls.

As the Danvers men reached the road the British would pass upon, one contingent of them entered an enclosure formed by the low stone walls bordering the Jason Russell property. They were apparently under the command of Gideon Foster, a twenty-six-year-old captain of no combat experience. Coburn lists Foster

---

[17] James Duncan Phillips, <u>Salem in the Eighteenth Century</u>, Essex Institute, Salem, Massachusetts, 1969, p. 363.

in his rolls as a Second Lieutenant in Captain Epes' Company, but according to Danvers historian Richard B. Trask, Foster was given command of a newly-formed minute company ten days earlier.[18]

In any event, some of Foster's men piled the shingles they found in Jason Russell's yard into a kind of breastwork to provide better protection than that offered by the low stone walls. Captain Foster with another contingent of his men, took up a position outside of the enclosure on a hillside where some trees provided a little cover. Foster was warned by Captain Hutchinson to be alert for the flank guard, but he was apparently satisfied with the positions in which his men were deployed.[19]

As mentioned there were a number of men from Beverly and Lynn near the Danvers position, and as the British column approached in the road, the Essex County men opened fire. As their attention was focused on the British column, the citizen-soldiers were surprised by the sudden appearance of a strong British flank guard, which swept down upon them from the high ground to the right of the road. The men of Essex County were now caught between the fire of the main body of troops in the road and the flankers in their rear. From his position on the hillside, Captain Foster was able to escape, but his men in the enclosure along with some Beverly and Lynn men, as well as a Salem baker and others including Jason Russell, had no place to seek shelter except for the nearby house of Mr. Russell.

Some of the men who entered the front door of the Jason Russell house either ran to the upper chambers on the second level or they fled to the cellar. Those who sought safety on the second floor were slain by the British soldiers who pursued them upstairs. The eight or so Danvers, Beverly, and Lynn men who sought safety in the cellar had better luck. As soon as they

---

[18] Richard B. Trask, Danvers Gazette, Vol. 1 No. 1, Danvers Bicentennial Committee, Danvers, 1975, p. 3.

[19] Ellen Chase, The Beginnings of the American Revolution, Vol. III, Sir Isaac Pitman and Sons, Ltd., London, 1911, p. 130.

reached the cellar, the Essex County men reloaded their muskets and aimed them upwards at the doorway opening to the cellar stairs. One British soldier foolishly tried to descend the cellar stairs and paid for his mistake with his life. His fellow soldiers profited by his example and left the Americans in the cellar alone.[20]

A few of the colonials on the first-floor level tried to escape the house by jumping out the windows. Thirty-seven year old Daniel Townsend of Lynn leaped through the end window taking the sash with him, but he was shot dead by the soldiers. His Lynn comrade-in-arms, Timothy Munroe, followed Townsend through the window and took a ball through the leg, but managed to escape. His clothes and hat were pierced many times by bullets, but he lived to tell the story.[21]

In addition to the Americans killed within the Jason Russell House, there were a number of men cut down outside on the grounds. The owner of the house, Jason Russell, was shot down as he reached his front door. His body was pierced many times by bayonets as the soldiers stabbed his prone form on their way in and out of his house. Reuben Kennison of Beverly's Ryal Side section was shot and bayoneted many times in the yard of Jason Russell. Perley Putnam of Danvers was also killed in the Russell yard. One Danvers man, Jotham Webb, was killed while wearing his wedding clothes. According to the Danvers tradition, Webb, who had married only a few weeks earlier, upon hearing of the alarm donned his wedding clothes with the remark, "If I die, I will die in my best cloths."[22]

Nineteen year old Dennis Wallis of Danvers was one of those captured by the British near the Jason Russell house. The red-coated soldiers disarmed him and took his watch and his money.

---

[20] D. Hamilton Hurd, <u>History of Middlesex County Massachusetts</u>, J. W. Lewis and Co., Philadelphia, 1890, p. 180.

[21] Chase, p. 132.

[22] Harriet Silvester Tapley, <u>Chronicles of Danvers (Old Salem Village) 1632-1923</u>, The Danvers Historical Society, Danvers, Massachusetts, 1923, p. 72.

When the British started to kill some of the men they had captured, young Wallis became fearful for his life and fled. According to the Danvers tradition, he was hit 12 times by musket balls and left for dead. He didn't die, however, and was taken back to Danvers by his comrades-in-arms.[23]

The fact that the British killed some of their prisoners at the Jason Russell property is recorded by the eyewitness account of Captain Gideon Foster. According to Captain Foster:

"The men in the enclosure made a gallant resistance but were overpowered by numbers--some sought shelter in a neighboring house, and three or four, after they had surrendered themselves prisoners of war, were butchered with savage barbarity."[24]

There is no question that the fighting at the Jason Russell house and yard was vicious in its intensity and that the bayonet was frequently employed at close quarters by the British soldiers. The killing of prisoners was probably a reflection not only of rage, but also of the frustration the British soldiers felt toward their enemies who fired at them from the shelter provided by the homes, stone walls, trees, and other natural cover of the New England countryside. It should also be pointed out that prisoners presented the hard-pressed flankers with a problem as it would require that men be assigned to escort them to the main column on the road, and the flanking parties would be reduced by the number of men required to guard the prisoners. To simply disarm them and leave them was a poor alternative as the Americans could have re-armed themselves with the many muskets of the dead and seriously-wounded men who had fallen in the vicinity.

Captain Gideon Foster was able to withdraw from his position on the hillside, but he and his men, along with others from the Lynn and Needham companies, were forced towards

---

[23] Trask, p. 4.

[24] Ibid., p. 3.

Spy Pond to the eastward. During the fighting he later remarked that, "I discharged my musket at the enemy a number of times, I think eleven, with two balls each time and with well directed aim."[25] Foster went on to say that his comrade Nathaniel Cleaves of Beverly had his finger and ramrod cut away by an enemy shot. Foster also added, "Whether my shots took effect, I cannot say; but this I can say, if they did not it was not for the want of determined purpose, in him who sent them."[26] Captain Gideon Foster went on to live a long life and upon his death on November 1, 1845, he was, according to Harriet S. Tapley, the last surviving commissioned American officer of the Revolutionary War. He was given a military funeral with the respect due to a man who had attained the rank of Major-General after long years of service to his country.[27]

The road as it wound through the town of Menotomy was to be the scene of some of the heaviest fighting of the day. In addition to the Americans who had followed the British on their return march through Concord, Lincoln, and Lexington, many other minute and militia companies entered the fighting in Menotomy. In addition to the previously mentioned nine companies from Danvers, Coburn's muster rolls indicate that the following contingents entered the contest in Menotomy: two companies from Brookline, one company from Watertown, one company from Medford, one company from Malden, three companies from Roxbury, eight companies from Dedham, three companies from Needham, five companies from Lynn, three companies from Beverly, and one company from Menotomy. If Coburn's rolls are correct, the 37 companies that entered the contest in Menotomy contained almost 1800 men. These companies combined with the men who had followed the British

---

[25] Ibid.

[26] Ibid.

[27] Tapley, p. 80.

through the preceding three towns, presented a great danger to Lord Percy's embattled command.

There were many acts of individual heroism on April 19, 1775, but one act has been recorded by almost all the historians who have written on the subject. This involves the deeds of old Captain Samuel Whittemore, which occurred near the stretch of road between the Jason Russell house and the center of Menotomy. According to Coburn, this half mile section of road "proved to be the bloodiest half mile of all the Battle Road." Coburn wrote that 20 or more Americans and at least as many or more Britons were killed along this half mile. If Coburn's figures are correct, about 40 percent of the American fatalities on April 19, 1775 occurred in Menotomy along the half mile of road from the Jason Russell house to Menotomy Center.[28]

Captain Sam Whittemore could have stayed at home that Wednesday and his absence from the ranks would not have been missed by anyone. At eighty years of age, no one expected him to arm himself for battle. In his younger days, Captain Whittemore had been a militia officer, but his advanced age excused him from all military duties in 1775. Upon hearing news of the alarm early that morning, Mrs. Whittemore prepared to flee to her son's house near the Mystic River. She was surprised to see the old soldier oiling his musket and brace of pistols, and sharpening his sword. She begged him to accompany her to safety but he refused saying simply that he was going "up town."[29]

Captain Whittemore arrived along the route the British would pass before their appearance and carefully selected his position behind a stone wall in the rear of Cooper's Tavern by a crossroad to Woburn. He was in this position when he saw five British soldiers of the flank guard bearing down on him. Too old to run and of a determined nature, he decided to fight it out with the soldiers. Taking aim with his musket, he shot one of the advancing flankers in the breast. He brought down another with

---

[28] Coburn, p. 140.

[29] Ibid., p. 141.

a shot from one of his two pistols. Firing the other pistol he brought down a third redcoat. He was then hit in the face by a ball which carried away part of his cheek-bone. The remaining flankers were on him in an instant and bayoneted him repeatedly with savage fury at one who had shot their comrades.[30]

In normal circumstances, Captain Whittemore's life should have terminated under the violent British bayonet assault. This was not the case, however, and life lingered in his bloodied body when he was found some time later. He was carried to the Cooper Tavern where Doctor Simon Tufts of Medford stated that it was useless to dress the many wounds Captain Whittemore had received. Finally, however, his bullet wound and 13 bayonet wounds were attended to and the old man lived for almost another 18 years.[31] During the course of his recovery, he was asked if he was sorry he had gone out on April 19. "No," the remarkable New Englander replied, "I should do just so again!"[32] Some time later after the British had returned to Boston, a Boston woman overheard a British soldier say, "We killed an old devil there in Menotomy, but we paid almost too dear for it, lost three of our men, the last died this morning."[33]

There are a number of Americans besides old Captain Samuel Whittemore who are credited in various historians' accounts with multiple kills of British soldiers on April 19, 1775. As earlier mentioned, Sergeant John Ford of Chelmsford is credited with killing five Britons. Another such individual was Hezekiah Wyman of Woburn. Mounted on a white horse, Wyman stayed close to the British rear guard. Riding within gun range he would dismount and fire using his saddle as a gun rest. He apparently killed at least two flankers in the Menotomy fighting. He was apparently a man of some years as he was described as a gray

---

[30] Chase, p. 147.

[31] Ibid.

[32] Ibid.

[33] Ibid., p. 148.

haired hunter. Another mounted American who gave the British trouble was old Timothy Fuller of Middleton. Fuller was also mounted on a white horse. It was reported that after firing at the British, Fuller would ride back to his comrades who would provide him with a loaded musket. He would then ride within range again for another shot at the King's troops.[34]

As the British made their way through Menotomy, a tragic incident occurred in the Cooper Tavern, which has been recorded in about all of the historical accounts. Inside the tavern, landlord Benjamin Cooper and his wife Rachel had been mixing flip at the bar for two customers, Jason Winship, about forty-five years of age, and his brother-in-law, forty year old Jabez Wyman. Apparently, these unarmed civilians felt that the passing British soldiers posed them no danger. They were wrong. As the British drew near the tavern, they opened fire on it, sending musket balls crashing through the windows. Soldiers, probably flankers, burst into the tavern with fixed bayonets. Benjamin Cooper and his wife fled to safety in the cellar, but the two middle-aged flip drinkers, Winship and Wyman, were caught by the enraged soldiers in the first floor room. According to the deposition of Benjamin and Rachel Cooper dated May 10, 1775, the two customers, who the Coopers described as "aged gentlemen" were in fact

"immediately, most barbarously and inhumanly murdered by them: being stabbed through in many places, their heads mauled, skulls broke, and their brains dashed out on the floor and walls of the house; and further say not."[35]

As the British passed through Menotomy, they made several attempts to burn down houses along the road, but they were so closely pressed by the Provincials that they did not have time to

---

[34] Ibid., pp. 156-157.

[35] Cooper, Benjamin and Rachel, Deposition, The Journals of each Provincial Congress of Massachusetts in 1774 and 1775 and of the Committee of Safety with an Appendix, Dutton and Wentworth, Boston, 1838, p. 678.

fan the flames into real conflagrations. The British, for example, entered the Thomas home where they ripped the beds open, split up the furniture, and set the building on fire. The flames, however, were put out after they left. They also killed a horse in the stable and some hogs they found in the hog pen of the Thomas family. According to the traditional account, the British even fired at Mrs. Thomas as she fled the home carrying a child of two years in her arms. Two balls passed through her cap, but the woman escaped unhurt.[36]

If Frank Coburn's figures are correct, about half the Americans killed on the first day of the war were killed in Menotomy. He lists as killed in Menotomy seven men from Danvers, five men from Needham, four men from Lynn, three men from Menotomy, two men from Medford, and one each from the following towns: Beverly, Dedham, Salem, and Watertown for a total of 25 men.[37]

As Americans wounded in Menotomy, Coburn lists three men from Beverly, two men from Danvers, two men from Needham, and one each from Menotomy and Dedham for a total of nine men.[38] The higher percentage ratio of American killed to wounded in Menotomy is probably a reflection of the active role the British flankers played with their deadly bayonets. It is difficult to survive a bayonet attack, especially if one is stabbed repeatedly, although Captain Samuel Whittemore is a notable exception to this rule.

According to Coburn, the British had about 40 men killed in Menotomy on April 19, 1775, which represents over half of the men they would lose in the fighting that day.[39]

One tragic scene which those who viewed it would long remember, occurred in the Jason Russell house. After the British

---

[36] Chase, pp. 152-153.

[37] Coburn, pp. 143-144.

[38] Ibid., p. 144.

[39] Ibid., p. 144.

had passed, the Americans who were killed in and around the
Jason Russell house were carried inside the dwelling where they
were laid out, side by side, in the south room where their blood
merged to form a common pool on the gore-soaked floor.[40]
Among the bodies placed there was that of the master of the
house, Jason Russell, who died in defense of his property in the
truest sense.

Twelve of the twenty-five Americans who were killed in
Menotomy were placed on an oxen-drawn sled and transported
to the village churchyard where they were buried in a large grave
side by side.[41] Others were taken back for burial in their home
towns by their more fortunate surviving comrades-in-arms. A
young girl in Danvers, Joanna Mansfield, recalled that on April
20, 1775, she saw the bodies of the seven slain Danvers men as
they passed by in a cart. She noted that they all wore gray
homespun stockings. On Friday they were buried from the Old
South Church in Danvers with two minute companies of Salem
as escort with reversed arms and muffled drums. On the way to
the burial ground, the funeral procession met Provincial soldiers
from Newburyport, Salisbury, and Amesbury who were on their
way to join in the siege of Boston. These northern Essex County
men formed their ranks in a single line along the road as the
funeral passed. Three volleys were fired at the grave in honor of
those who had given their lives for the Patriot cause.[42]

When the British left Menotomy they left their dead and
some of their more seriously wounded men behind. Among the
latter was Lt. Edward Hull of the British 43rd Regiment of Foot.
He was first wounded at the North Bridge in Concord and was
placed in a chaise for the ride back. This chaise was probably the
one that was commandeered from Mr. Reuben Brown of
Concord. While riding in the chaise he received two more

---

[40] Ibid., p. 140.

[41] Ibid., p. 144.

[42] Chase, pp. 136-137.

musket balls in the body. He was taken to the Butterfield house in Menotomy on the north side of the road not far from Cooper's Tavern. While at the Butterfield home, Lt. Hull was visited by a Reverend McClure who described him as "of a youthful, fair and delicate countenance." Rev. McClure noted that the young officer had no shirt on, and was wrapped in a great coat with a fur cap on his head. The Reverend inquired why the young man was so destitute of clothing. Lt. Hull answered "When I fell, our people stripped me of my coat, vest and shirt, and your people of my shoes and buckles." From his countenance, Rev. McClure perceived that the officer was in great pain from his three wounds. Lt. Edward Hull lingered in this life until May 2, 1775. After his passing, in deference to his request, his body was taken to the Charlestown Ferry where a barge from the Somerset carried him to Boston where he was buried far from his comfortable home and kin in Scotland.[43]

From time to time the British fired their cannon to prevent the Americans from massing and overpowering Percy's rear guard. Their supply of cannon balls was limited, however, and was running dangerously low in Menotomy. Despite the threat of Percy's cannon, the Provincials pressed close to Percy's rear, which was protected by the battalion companies of the 23rd Regiment (Royal Welch Fusiliers). The Royal Welch was hit hard in Menotomy and their wounded included the regiment's field commander, Lt. Col. Benjamin Bernard, who was wounded in the thigh. At some point in Menotomy, Percy relieved the bloodied 23rd Regiment with the 1st Battalion of Marines. The Marines covered the rear during some of the bloodiest fighting of the day. Due to their dangerous position in the column, the Marines took heavy casualties. By the end of the day, Major Pitcairn's Marines suffered 31 men killed, 38 men wounded, 3 officers wounded, and 2 men missing. The Marine casualties were the highest that any British unit suffered on April 19, 1775.

It was between five and six o'clock that the Imperial troops approached the Menotomy River separating Menotomy from

---

[43] Ibid., pp. 148-150.

Cambridge. In Menotomy, the King's men had been under the most heavy fire that they had encountered that day. They continued to move forward, however, with their main body in the road and their flanking parties out on each side. The wounded made a pitiful sight, some limping along, others clinging to horses. Ensign Jeremy Lister, who had been wounded earlier in the day at Meriam's Corner, described his experience in the Menotomy area as follows:

"When I had rode about two miles I found the balls whistled so smartly about my ears I thought it more prudent to dismount and as the balls came thicker from one side or the other so I went from one side of the horse to the other for some time when a horse was shot dead close by me, that had a wounded man on his back and three hanging by his sides, they immediately begged the assistance of my horse which I readily granted, and soon after left him wholly to their care."[44]

The British passage through Menotomy had been costly to both sides as each had suffered more casualties in that town than in any other community along the Battle Road. The Menotomy fighting was also characterized by a vicious "no quarter asked, no quarter given" style that was probably as rough as any fighting of the war. The high ratio of American killed to wounded in Menotomy lends support to this and also to the American statements that the British were killing some of those unfortunates who tried to surrender to them. In any event, Percy's men passed over the Menotomy River (Alewife Brook) and into Cambridge between five and six o'clock. They were badly bloodied, but were still intact as a fighting force.

---

[44] Ensign Jeremy Lister, <u>Concord Fight</u>, Harvard University, Cambridge, Massachusetts, 1931, pp. 31-32.

9 - RETURN THROUGH CAMBRIDGE INTO CHARLESTOWN TO BUNKER HILL

As Percy crossed the Menotomy River into Cambridge, his strong flanking parties had been reduced by the casualties they had taken in Lexington and Menotomy. Perhaps equally or even more detrimental to the efficiency of his flanking parties was the tendency of these Light Infantry soldiers to waste time in looting the private homes they entered on each side of the road.

Percy's rear guard appeared to be effective, thanks to the respect the colonials held for the two six-pound field pieces. Percy also instituted a policy of changing his rear guard so no one unit had to serve in this dangerous position for the entire march back. The British could only fire their cannon occasionally as they were very low on ammunition. According to Ensign Jeremy Lister's account, Colonel Cleveland, the artillery commander, sent only seven rounds of ammunition for each gun. In his defense, Cleveland later said that Percy, fearing that he might be delayed by baggage, limited the supply of ball to only that which could be transported in the side-boxes.[1] According to the account of Lt. William Sutherland of His Majesty's 38th

---

[1] Ensign Jeremy Lister, <u>Concord Fight</u>, Harvard University Press, Cambridge, 1931, p. 30.

Regiment of Foot, the British were actually out of cannon shots in Menotomy. Sutherland stated: "We were most annoyed at a village called Anatomy, having no shot to fire from our cannon on the houses which were full of men of which we killed a great number."[2] The Americans, of course, could not be sure of the status of the ammunition for the cannon, and consequently, they continued to show great respect for the two six-pounders.

It was not far from the Menotomy River on the Cambridge side that another of a number of individual confrontations that are recorded on April 19, 1775 occurred. Lt. Solomon Bowman of Captain Benjamin Locke's 53-man Menotomy Militia Company overtook a British straggler. Each man's musket was unloaded at the time of their meeting. The Briton advanced at Bowman with fixed bayonet, but the lieutenant deflected it and felled his opponent with the butt end of his musket. Bowman than took the Redcoat prisoner.[3]

Further on in Cambridge, a number of armed Americans gathered near the home of Jacob Watson located on the southerly side of the road. They had grouped behind a pile of empty casks where they waited for the British to come into range. With their attention focused on the road, the colonials did not notice the British flankers, who had come up in their rear until it was too late. The flankers opened fire and three citizen-soldiers were killed near Watson's residence.[4]

The armed patriots killed near Watson's were Major Isaac Gardner of Brookline, and two Cambridge men, John Hicks, about fifty years old, and fifty-three year old Moses Richardson.[5]

[2] Lt. William Sutherland, narrative contained in Late News of the Excursion and Ravages of the King's Troops on the Nineteenth of April 1775, Harvard College Press, Cambridge, 1927, p. 24.

[3] Frank Warren Coburn, The Battle of April 19, 1775, F. L. Coburn and Co., Boston, 1912, pp. 145-146.

[4] Ibid., pp. 147-148.

[5] Ibid.

Another Cambridge man, William Marcy, was also killed not far from Watson's. According to tradition, Marcy, an unarmed civilian, was sitting on a fence, probably enjoying the exciting scene that was unfolding before his eyes. His enjoyment was cut short as his life was terminated by a British musket ball. It was said at the time that Marcy was feeble-minded, and he probably thought he was watching a sham fight such as the militia occasionally put on in those days.[6]

The forty-nine year old major from Brookline, Isaac Gardner, was the first Harvard graduate to be killed in the war. His body was pretty well torn open by the entry of many musket balls and bayonet thrusts. His seventeen year old son, also named Isaac, was nearby as the young man was a fifer in Captain Thomas White's Brookline Militia Company. Major Gardner was quite prominent in Brookline having held the offices of justice of the peace, school committeeman, town surveyor, and town clerk. He also left a widow and eight children.[7]

John Hicks, Moses Richardson, and William Marcy were all buried by torchlight on the night of April 19, 1775 in a common grave. Richardson's son Elias jumped into the trench and spread the cape of his coat over his father's face so that the dirt would not fall directly on it. Major Gardner's body was found under an apple tree near the road. He was secretly buried on the second night after the battle in Brookline to, according to Ellen Chase, "prevent the agony the sight would have occasioned his countrymen."[8]

The British seem to have had the best of the fighting near Watson's residence, but at least one soldier of the King lost his life in that vicinity. According to Edmund Foster, who came upon the scene sometime after the British had passed:

---

[6] Samuel Adams Drake, History of Middlesex County, Massachusetts, Estes and Lauriat, Boston, 1880, p. 344.

[7] Ellen Chase, The Beginnings of the American Revolution, Vol. III, Sir Isaac Pitman and Sons, Ltd., London, 1911, pp. 158-159.

[8] Ibid., p. 159.

> *"At Snow's, now Davenports' Tavern in Cambridge, one of the enemy lay dead by the road, and directly opposite, one of our best men, Major Gardner of Brookline was killed, and his death much lamented."*[9]

In addition to Major Gardner, two other leading Brookline men took part in the Cambridge fighting. These were Colonel Thomas Aspinwall and his brother, Dr. William Aspinwall. The latter had first donned his red coat, but later changed it when it was suggested that he might be mistaken for a British soldier. Dr. Aspinwall was blind in one eye and was forced to aim from his left shoulder. According to the traditional story, Dr. Aspinwall dropped a British soldier with a well-aimed musket ball. A fellow patriot, Ebenezer Davis, remarked to the doctor that the downed Redcoat's musket was fair spoil, but the good doctor had no time to gather muskets from the dead. Without pausing he continued his useful chase of the enemy. Dr. William Aspinwall later married one of the daughters of his fallen comrade-in-arms, Major Isaac Gardner.[10]

Ahead of Percy's column the road forked with the right side going to Cambridge and the left side going to Charlestown. Under Percy's orders the column turned left at the fork rather than continuing on the road which would take them to the bridge spanning the Charles River in Cambridge. Percy's decision to take the road to Charlestown was probably the best decision he made that day. Had he returned by the way he came out, he would have had to fight his way through the large body of militia waiting for him on the Cambridge road leading to the bridge. Even if he got through the militia to the bridge, he would have found it impassable as General Heath had ordered the planks removed. Moreover, darkness was closing in. According to Low's Almanack, the sun set at seven o'clock on April 19, 1775. At this

---

[9] Edmund Foster, account contained in A History of the Fight at Concord on the 19th of April 1775 by the Rev. Ezra Ripley, D.D., Allen and Atwell, Concord, 1927, p. 36.

[10] Chase, pp. 158-159.

point Percy had less than an hour of daylight left. Darkness was no friend of the British that day. Their enemies were hard enough to see in the daylight. The Charlestown road offered Lord Percy the shortest route to the high ground where he could deploy his troops in a good defensive position. From there he could also receive the support of the Army in nearby Boston and the guns of the Royal Navy, whose ships could be brought within gun range of Charlestown.

As his column veered eastward down the road to Charlestown, Percy could see a large body of colonial militia waiting for him on the other road to Cambridge. To keep the militia off his right flank as the column turned left, Percy ordered his cannon to fire at the colonials. According to Percy's own statement:

"During the whole of our retreat, the rebels endeavored to annoy us by concealing themselves behind stone walls and within houses and firing straggling shot at us from thence; nor did I during the whole time perceive any body of them drawn up together, except near Cambridge, just as we turned down towards Charlestown, who dispersed on a cannon shot being fired at them, and came down to attack our right flank in the same straggling manner the rest had done before."[11]

Percy's statement that a cannon shot was fired at the body of men near Cambridge as his column turned toward Charlestown is at odds with Lt. Sutherland's remark that the British were out of cannon shot to fire at the men in the houses in Menotomy. Perhaps the British in Menotomy were saving their few rounds to fire only at large bodies of men near the road, which Percy might have considered a more dangerous threat than the smaller groups of men concealed in the individual houses. In any event, Sutherland apparently was unaware of the cannon being fired in Cambridge as the road, turned toward Charlestown.

---

[11] Lord Hugh Earl Percy, Report to General Gage dated April 20, 1775, Contained in <u>Letters of Hugh Earl Percy from Boston and New York, 1774-1776</u>, Ed. by Charles Knowles Bolton, Charles E. Goodspeed, Boston, 1902, p. 51.

According to Coburn, Percy fired his cannon again in Cambridge further on down the road from a hill in the rear of Timothy Tufts' home. Again, no one was killed by this cannon discharge, but a number of Britons were killed by a scattering fire directed at them by Americans positioned in a grove of trees up the road. Coburn stated that the British soldiers fell in the road near the Tufts residence.[12] It may be that these Regulars were killed by the Americans who Percy described as attacking his right flank in a straggling manner shortly after his cannon fired in Cambridge.

Coburn estimates the time of the fighting near the Timothy Tufts home to be about 6:30 p.m. Shortly after the British passed the Tufts home they came to a little pond and many of the King's troops jumped in to cool off. Others laying prone along the edge of the pond drank its refreshing waters. Beyond the pond, the road went along the westerly foot of Prospect Hill. Here, according to Coburn, more Britons were killed and Percy once more fired his field pieces at the Americans.[13]

As the British continued along, they came to the home of Samuel Shed on the northerly side of the road. One of the soldiers entered the Shed home and seeing a highboy he opened a drawer and started to sift through its contents. With his attention engaged by the items in the drawer, the Briton probably never saw the American who fired the musket whose ball ended his life. Three other musket balls penetrated the highboy, which was spattered with the luckless looter's blood.[14]

Further down the road, along the slope of Prospect Hill, sixty-five year old James Miller opened fire on the British as they came into range. Apparently Miller got off a number of shots before the British discovered his position. A party of soldiers headed in Miller's direction. Miller's companion urged him to

---

[12] Coburn, p. 150.

[13] Ibid., p. 152.

[14] Ibid., pp. 152-153.

run, but the elderly patriot declared "I am too old to run." The Regulars opened fire and the citizen-soldier fell with, according to the traditional story, 13 musket ball wounds in his body.[15] A tablet, which was later erected near the scene, read as follows:

On this Hillside James Miller minuteman aged 65 was slain by the British April 19, 1775 "I am too old to run"

The reader should not be surprised by the advanced age of James Miller. At various points in the day's fighting, the British were harassed by Massachusetts men over fifty years of age. These old fighters appear to share a common trait. They would choose a position near the road and from there they would make their stand. They either could not effectively or would not run in the face of the enemy. Examples of this are illustrated by the actions of Jonas Parker on Lexington Common, Captain Samuel Whittemore of Menotomy, and, of course, James Miller.

At the foot of Prospect Hill a Redcoat was shot as he was about to enter a house. In addition, his body was bayoneted. His lifeless form was later found in the grass by men of the Malden Company as they pursued the British.[16]

Pressed for time and with darkness closing in, the British did not have time to fan the flames of many fires in this vicinity. Ebenezer Shed lost his house and several outbuildings, and the property of the slain James Miller was damaged.[17] As the British column passed the Prospect Hill area, they were observed by Col. Timothy Pickering of Salem who, with a portion of his First Essex Regiment, had reached the summit of Winter Hill about a mile to the northeast.[18] Historian Richard Frothingham estimated that Col. Pickering had about 700 men with him, but James Duncan Phillip's estimate of 300 is probably closer to the

---

[15] Chase, p. 167.

[16] Ibid., p. 173.

[17] Coburn, pp. 150-154.

[18] Richard Frothingham, History of the Siege of Boston, Little Brown and Company, Boston, 1896, p. 78.

truth.[19] It must be remembered that a large portion of Pickering's Regiment from Danvers had arrived earlier in Menotomy to take part in some of the bitterest fighting of the day under the leadership of the Danvers captains. The Marblehead contingent of Pickering's regiment was also absent as the selectmen of Marblehead kept their militia at home to protect the town from a possible British attack from sea.

Col. Timothy Pickering enjoyed an excellent military reputation locally, but the portion of his regiment that he commanded on Winter Hill was too far from the British column to strike at it. Pickering and his men could only watch in frustration as the British passed on down the road to Charlestown. Among those Salem men who watched helplessly from Winter Hill as the British approached Charlestown was one of Salem's most active maritime merchants, Elias Hasket Derby. On this day Mr. Derby was serving as a common private in the ranks of one of the Salem companies. He would later go on to become one of America's leading privateer owners during the Revolutionary War.

At the time and later after he entered politics, Col. Pickering was criticized by some for what his critics called his tardy arrival on the scene of battle on April 19, 1775. His defenders pointed out that the men from Danvers, whose route to the battle road was some three or so miles shorter than what Pickering had to march, barely arrived in time to engage the British in Menotomy. They also noted that some towns nearer to the British route than Salem failed to send men in time to engage the British. In any event, Col. Pickering and the Salem companies were completely vindicated by a resolution of the Provincial Congress in August of 1775.[20]

Colonel Timothy Pickering went on to become one of General George Washington's most trusted and able officers during the Revolutionary War. After leading his regiment in the

[19] James Duncan Phillips, Salem in the Eighteenth Century, Essex Institute, 1969, p. 363.

[20] Ibid., pp. 363-364.

New York campaign of early 1777, Pickering in April was appointed by Washington to the post of Adjutant-General. In 1780, Washington appointed Pickering to the post of Quartermaster-General where he served with efficiency and distinction. After the Revolutionary War, General Pickering served the new Republic as Secretary of State from 1795 to 1800 and represented Massachusetts in the United States Senate from 1803 to 1811. In politics he was a strong Federalist.

As the British crossed the line into Charlestown, they marched quickly to the common and turned to the right up the slope to Bunker Hill. It was near the common that another tragic event involving a civilian occurred. In the home of William Barber, a sea captain, one of his 13 children, Edward, only fourteen years old, sat at a window watching the British troops pass along the nearby road. One of the Redcoats pointed his musket at the young boy and pulled the trigger. Young Edward fell back into the room dead, thus becoming the only person from Charlestown to die on April 19, 1775.[21]

The British did not meet any organized resistance from the Charlestown citizens who, due to their nearness to the main army in Boston and the King's Navy, were forced to sign an agreement that they would not attack the British and would also provide them aid in getting across the river to Boston. In return, the British agreed not to attack the citizens or destroy their homes.[22]

Once they reached the high ground of Bunker Hill, the exhausted British soldiers were relatively safe. The high ground provided a good defensive position, which could be supported by the guns of the Royal Navy. The Regulars were also near to their main army in Boston where they could be reinforced by troops brought over the Charles by the Navy.

According to Lord Hugh Earl Percy's official account to General Thomas Gage, his command reached Charlestown

---

[21] Coburn, p. 155.

[22] Ibid., pp. 155-156.

between 7 and 8 p.m. on the fateful Wednesday evening. He wrote that his men were "very much fatigued with a march of above 30 miles and having expended almost all our ammunition."[23]

Upon reaching Bunker Hill, Lord Percy deployed a line across the narrow neck of land leading to the high ground and positioned his men in defensive positions on the hill. He also sent a message over the river to General Gage in Boston requesting immediate ammunition and reinforcements. General Heath, upon seeing Percy's deployment, decided that the British were in too strong a defensive position to successfully attack, and he gave orders to the American minute and militia companies, which had reached the Charlestown common area not to attack, as he believed that any attack on the enemy in their strong defensive position would be futile.[24]

General William Heath soon gathered his officers around him at the foot of Prospect Hill and ordered a guard to be posted there. He also ordered sentinels to be stationed near the Neck and patrols to reconnoiter during the night. He left instructions that the patrols report any movement of the enemy to him during the night. He then ordered the Provincial forces to march to Cambridge where they were told to "lie on their arms."[25] The stage was thus set for the next phase of the war, which was the siege of Boston.

The British on Bunker Hill were soon reinforced by additional soldiers sent over from Boston on boats. These fresh troops also brought over supplies of ammunition. After the reinforcements, ammunition, and whatever other supplies were unloaded, the boats returned to Boston with the wounded. The exhausted men who had constituted Lt. Col. Francis Smith's

---

[23] Percy, p. 50.

[24] William Heath, Memoirs of Major General William Heath, William Abbatt, New York, 1901, p. 9.

[25] Ibid.

command were also taken over to Boston on the boats. Percy's men remained on the hill. Soldiers from the 10th Regiment with pickets from the 2nd and 3rd brigades, including a detachment from the 64th, came over and were posted on the heights and the Neck. According to Lt. Mackenzie, the last regiment that went on the march did not return to their barracks until after midnight. The soldiers who remained on the hill were in the act of building a redoubt when General Gage gave orders for the redoubt to be demolished and Charlestown abandoned. According to Mackenzie, the troops were back in Boston by 4 p.m. on April 20.[26]

British casualties were heavy on April 19, 1775. As a result of wounds suffered on that day, 73 of the King's Regulars would lose their lives including two officers who later died, Lt. Knight and Lt. Hull. They also had 174 men wounded including at least 15 officers. Two of the wounded officers were regimental commanders, Lt. Col. Francis Smith of the 10th Regiment and Lt. Col. Bery Bernard of the 23rd Regiment. The British also listed 26 men missing for a total of 273 casualties.[27]

By far the hardest hit of the British units was the marines who suffered 74 casualties including two officers, Captain Souter and Lt. McDonald. One officer, Lt. Potter, was listed as missing. Most of the marine casualties probably occurred after the marines took over the rear guard position from the Royal Welch Fusiliers, which was, according to Lt. Mackenzie, some seven miles from where Percy started his return march from Lexington. Mackenzie also stated that the Marines were relieved from the dangerous rear guard position by the 47th Regiment who, in turn, were relieved by the 4th Regiment.[28]

---

[26] Lt. Frederick Mackenzie, Diary account published in <u>A British Fusilier in Revolutionary Boston</u>, Harvard University Press, 1926, pp. 67-69.

[27] Coburn, pp. 159-160.

[28] Mackenzie, p. 57.

It is interesting to note that the four units that rotated in Percy's rear guard, the 23rd Regiment, the marines, the 47th Regiment, and the 4th Regiment suffered, according to Gage's return, upwards of 180 total casualties, a high percentage for the day. Of course, the men from the 4th Regiment were also hard hit at Concord's North Bridge. It should be mentioned that Gage's return was lower than the actual number of British casualties.

The American losses on April 19, 1775 consisted of 49 killed, 41 wounded and 5 missing for a total of 95.[29] It is interesting to compare the higher proportion of British wounded to killed with the American casualties, which indicate fewer colonials were wounded then killed. Contemporary authorities such as General William Heath pointed out that:

"It will also be observed that the wounded of the militia did not bear the common proportion with the killed, and is an evidence that the British did not choose to encumber themselves with prisoners, either wounded or not, as the marks left at Watson's Corners and on the height above Menotomy meeting-house evinced."[30]

The British did take some prisoners, however, as the following diary account of Lt. Frederick Mackenzie would indicate: "We brought in about ten prisoners, some of whom were taken in arms. One or two more were killed on the march while prisoners by the fire of their own people."[31]

On the American side, Lexington with its ten killed and ten wounded, had the most total casualties of any Massachusetts town whose men saw action on April 19, 1775. Next to Lexington, Danvers, whose men came further than any town

---

[29] Coburn, pp. 157-158.

[30] Heath, p. 9.

[31] Mackenzie, p. 58.

who engaged the British on that fateful Wednesday, suffered the most severely. Danvers lost seven killed and two wounded.

Discipline among the King's troops was not improved by the fact that 17 officers and 10 sergeants were listed among the casualties of the day. This lack of discipline and the tendency of British looters to linger in the homes along the roadside doubtless contributed to a higher casualty rate among the common soldiers. This was brought out in the reports given to General Gage by Lord Percy and other officers. General Gage reacted to the lack of discipline by issuing positive orders that "no man quit his rank to plunder or pillage, or to enter a house unless ordered to do so, under the pain of death, and each officer will be made answerable for the platoon under his command."[32] Gage's official report on the affair made no mention of the breakdown of discipline in the ranks on April 19, 1775, nor did the British acknowledge in public that a discipline problem existed. In the military, whenever a breakdown in discipline occurs, the quality of leadership normally comes under question. Therefore, it is sometimes better to not mention it in public, but to take steps to insure that the problem does not repeat itself. Apparently, this is the course that General Gage took.

Although the Battle of April 19, 1775 has always fascinated students of human nature and inspired American patriots, it has never been studied by military students to any extent as a classic model of military operations. As mentioned, the conduct of the professional British soldiers left much to be desired in the way of good order and discipline. Gage's plan to destroy the provincial supplies was flawed from the start by the lack of security and mistakes in implementation. The main bright spot from the British point of view relates to Acting Brigadier General Percy's conduct on his rescue mission to save Lt Col. Francis Smith and his detachment. Even Percy has been criticized, however, for his neglect in adequately protecting his baggage train and for his oversight in not insuring that he had enough ammunition for his cannon. American historians have also faulted Percy for not

---

[32] Ibid., p. 73.

doing more to prevent the looting of private property by his troops. Perhaps the strongest criticism of the plan General Gage and his staff devised to destroy the American arms and supplies came from the British officers involved in the actual implementation of it. In private accounts, some British officers, including Lt. William Mackenzie and Lt. John Barker were highly critical of the overall plan. Perhaps the following remark contained in Barker's diary best sums up his view on the subject: "Thus ended the expedition, which from beginning to end was ill planned and ill executed as it was possible to be."[33]

The American forces, on the other hand, were not a model of military perfection either. There was an absence of overall control to American operations. Coordination between units left much to be desired. Many Americans got separated from their companies and wound up fighting as individuals. In general, there was a lack of command and control on the American side, which prevented them from destroying or capturing the entire British force.

As individuals, the Americans were better adapted by attitude and experience to fight in the style that the tactical and terrain conditions along the Battle Road presented than the average British soldiers. The Briton, trained in the linear open-field warfare of Europe, found it difficult to cope with men who fired at him from concealed positions. In fact, many British soldiers considered the Massachusetts men to be cowards for not exchanging volleys with them out in the open.

There are many individual accounts of American bravery on April 19, 1775. Perhaps the most interesting observation on the individual American fighting man came from Lord Hugh Earl Percy himself. In a letter to General Harvey written the day after the battle Percy said,

"Nor are several of their men void of a spirit of enthusiasm, as we experienced yesterday, for many of them concealed themselves in houses, and

---

[33] Lt. John Barker, Diary account contained in <u>The British in Boston</u>, Harvard University Press, Cambridge, 1924, p. 37.

advanced within ten yards to fire at men and other officers, tho' they were morally certain of being put to death themselves in an instant."[34]

In view of the low esteem in which Percy held most Americans prior to April 19, 1775, his remark to General Harvey must be considered as a great compliment to his colonial adversaries.

Despite the command and control problems the Americans experienced on April 19, 1775, most historians considered the minute man concept a success. The network of alarm riders succeeded in alerting the far-flung local companies in time for many of them to make contact with the British. The story of the alarm riders is a tale in itself that deserves more space than this study can spare.

For more than a century and a half afterwards, proponents of a large state national guard system, as opposed to a large federal regular army, pointed to the American success on April 19, 1775 as justification for the part-time, citizen-soldier concept. On the other hand, proponents of the more expensive large federal regular army point out that better organized regular troops probably would have destroyed the British soldiers on April 19, 1775. By and large, however, the minute man/militia system of Massachusetts worked well enough on the first day of the war and to the conditions of Massachusetts over two centuries ago.

In the immediate aftermath of April 19, 1775, each side was eager to cast the blame on the other and to spread their version of the actual events. On April 22, 1775, the Provincial Congress meeting in Concord appointed a committee of eight, headed by Marblehead's Elbridge Gerry to take formal depositions from the battle participants and other eyewitnesses. People were interviewed and soon 20 signed affidavits authenticated by notarial certificates were gathered. The signed American affidavits, including two signed by captured British soldiers, indicated that the British fired first on Lexington Common and Concord's North Bridge. A letter in the form of an appeal to the

---

[34] Percy, p. 53.

inhabitants of Great Britain by Joseph Warren, the President pro tem of the Provincial Congress was included in the packet containing the letters. Warren especially wanted the letter and affidavits to reach the eyes of the Lord Mayor and the aldermen and councilmen of London.[35]

On April 27, Captain John Derby of Salem sailed from Salem aboard the 60-ton schooner Quero under sailing master William Carleton. Derby was under orders from the Committee of Safety to deliver the package of affidavits and Dr. Warren's letters to Benjamin Franklin, the agent for Massachusetts in London. Unknown to Captain Derby, Franklin was himself on the high seas en route to America. Speed was essential as four days earlier the ship Sukey of two hundred tons sailed from Boston carrying General Gage's report of the fighting on April 19, 1775.[36]

Captain John Derby reached London on May 28 and gave the acting provincial agent, Arthur Lee, his official documents including copies of the April 21 and April 25 Essex Gazette. The Quero must have been a fast-sailing schooner, as the Sukey, despite her four-day head start, arrived some days later when the news of April 19, 1775 was somewhat stale. After comparing the American and British accounts, the main issue for the British press appeared to be a discussion as to whether the British troops retreated or were routed on their return march to Boston.[37]

April 19, 1775, of course, marked the first clash of arms between the organized American militia and troops of the British Regular Army. In a larger sense, it proved to be the start of that long and bitter war that resulted in the formation and independence of the United States of America. Out of that same war, Britain lost 13 of her mainland colonies in North America,

---

[35] Phillips, pp. 365-366.

[36] Ibid., p. 366.

[37] Ibid., p. 368.

an occurrence of severe impact upon the British Empire and great influence on the course of modern world history.

BIBLIOGRAPHY

PRIMARY SOURCES: PUBLISHED LETTERS, JOURNALS, REPORTS, AND DEPOSITIONS

Bolton, Charles Knowles (ed.), Letters of Hugh Earl Percy, Boston and New York, 1774-1776, Charles E. Goodspeed, Boston, 1902.

Carter, Clarence Edwin (ed.), The Correspondence of General Thomas Gage with the Secretaries of State 1763-1775, Vol. l, Yale University Press, New Haven, 1931.

Clark, William Bell (ed.), Naval Documents of the American Revolution, Vol. I, 1774-1775, Superintendent of Documents, Washington, D. C., 1964.

Concord Fight: Being So Much of the Narrative of Ensign Jeremy Lister of the 10th Regiment of Foot as Pertains to his Services on the 19th of April 1775, and to his Experiences in Boston During the Early Months of the Siege, Harvard University Press, Cambridge, 1931.

Dana, Elizabeth Ellery (ed.), <u>The British in Boston: Being the Diary of Lieutenant John Barker of the King's Own Regiment from Nov. 15, 1774 to May 31, 1776</u>, Harvard University Press, Cambridge, 1924.

French, Allen, <u>General Gage's Informers</u>, "Captain Walter S. Laurie's Report to General Gage, April 26, 1775," The University of Michigan Press, Ann Arbor, 1932.

French, Allen (ed.), <u>A British Fusilier in Revolutionary Boston: Being the Diary of Lieutenant Frederick Mackenzie, Adjutant of the Royal Welch Fusiliers, Jan. 5 - April 30, 1775; With a Letter Describing His Voyage to America</u>, Harvard University Press, Cambridge, 1926.

French, Allen (ed.), <u>The Concord Fight</u>, "An Account by Amos Barrett," Thomas Todd Co., Boston, 1924.

Frothingham, Richard, <u>History of the Siege of Boston and of the Battles of Lexington, Concord and Bunker Hill</u>, "Petition of Martha Moulton, Feb. 4, 1776," Little Brown and Company, Boston, 1896.

<u>The Journals of Each Provincial Congress of Massachusetts in 1774 and 1775 and of the Committee of Safety with an Appendix</u>, "Deposition of Benjamin and Rachel Cooper," Dutton and Wentworth, Boston, 1839.

Kehoe, Vincent J. R. (ed.), <u>We Were There! The American Rebels</u>, "American Accounts," Chelmsford, Massachusetts, 1975.

Kehoe, Vincent J. R. (ed.), <u>We Were There! The British Soldiers</u>, "British Accounts," Chelmsford, Massachusetts, 1975.

Leighton, Hannah, <u>An Address Delivered at Acton July 21, 1835 Being the First Centennial Anniversary of the Organization of that Town with an Appendix</u>, Josiah Adams (ed.), "Deposition of the Wife of Capt. Isaac Davis," J. F. Buckingham, Boston, 1835.

<u>The Manual Exercise as Ordered by His Majesty in 1764 Together with Plans and Explanations at Reviews and Field Days</u>, F. and J. Fleet, Boston.

<u>Memoirs of Major-General William Heath</u>, William Abbatt, New York, 1901.

Moore, Frank (ed.), <u>The Diary of the American Revolution 1775-1781</u>, Washington Square Press, New York, 1967.

Murdock, Harold (ed.), <u>Late News of the Excursion and Ravages of the King's Troops on the Nineteenth of April 1775</u>, "Lt. William Sutherland's Narratives, April 26, 1775," Harvard Press, Cambridge, 1927.

<u>A Narrative of the Excursion and Ravages of the King's Troops Under the Command of General Gage on the 19th of April 1775; Together with the Depositions Taken by Order of Congress to Support the Truth of It</u>, Worcester, 1775.

Phinney, Elias, <u>History of the Battle at Lexington on the Morning of the 19th April 1775</u>, (Later American Depositions), Phelps and Farnham, Boston, 1825.

Revere, Paul, <u>Paul Revere's Three Accounts of His Famous Ride</u>, Massachusetts Historical Society, Boston, 1961.

Ripley, Ezra, <u>A History of the Fight at Concord, on the 19th of April 1775</u>, "Letter of Edmund Foster, dated March 10, 1825," Allen and Atwell, Concord, 1827.

Scull, G.D. (ed.), Memoir and Letters of Captain W. Glanville Evelyn of the 4th Regiment, from North America, 1774-1776, James Parker and Co., Oxford, 1879.

Upham, William P. (ed.), Letters Written at the Time of the Occupation of Boston, Essex Institute Historical Collections, Salem, Mass., 1876.

Willard, Margaret Wheeler (ed.), Letters on the American Revolution 1774-1776, Houghton Mifflin Co., Boston, 1925.

William Emerson's Diary, "Proceedings of the Centennial Celebration of Concord's Fight," Concord, 1876.

UNPUBLISHED PRIMARY SOURCES

Blood, Thaddeus, "Thaddeus Blood's Account of April 19, 1775," Concord Free Public Library, Concord, Massachusetts.

"Massachusetts State Archives, Vol. 138," p. 407, "Relating to the Plunder of the Ebenezer Fiske House."

SECONDARY SOURCES

Alden, John R., The American Revolution 1775-1783, Harper and Row, New York, 1954.

Brown, Abram English, Beneath Old Roof Trees, Lee and Shepard, Boston, 1896.

Brown, Louise K., A Revolutionary Town, Phoenix Publishing Co., Canaan, N.H., 1775.

Castle, Norman, The Minute Men, Yankee Colour Corporation, Southborough, Mass., 1977.

Chase, Ellen, The Beginnings of the American Revolution, Vol. III, Sir Isaac Pitman and Sons, Ltd., London, 1911.

Coburn, Frank Warren, The Battle of April 19, 1775, in Lexington, Concord, Lincoln, Arlington, Cambridge, Somerville and Charlestown, Massachusetts, F. L. Coburn and Co., Boston, 1912.

Coburn, Frank Warren, The Battle on Lexington Common: April 19, 1775, F. L. Coburn and Co., Boston, 1921.

Concord Chamber of Commerce, The Lexington-Concord Battle Road, Concord, Massachusetts.

Darling, Anthony D., Red Coat and Brown Bess, Museum Restoration Service, Bloomfield, Ontario, 1970.

Drake, Samuel Adams, History of Middlesex County, Estes and Lauriat, Boston, 1880.

Field, Edward, The Colonial Tavern, Preston and Rounds, Providence, 1897.

Forbes, Esther, Paul Revere and the World He Lived In, Houghton Mifflin Co., Boston, 1942.

French, Allen, The Day of Concord and Lexington, Little Brown, Boston, 1925.

French, Allen, General Gage's Informers, The University of Michigan Press, Ann Arbor, 1932.

Frey, Sylvia R., The British Soldiers in America, University of Texas Press, Austin, 1981.

Frothingham, Richard, <u>History of the Siege of Boston</u>, Little Brown and Co., Boston, 1896.

Galvin, John R., <u>The Minute Men</u>, Hawthorn Books Inc., New York, 1967.

Gooding, S. James, <u>An Introduction to British Artillery in North America</u>, Museum Restoration Service, Bloomfield, Ontario, 1980.

Gross, Robert A., <u>The Minute Men and Their World</u>, Hill and Wang, New York, 1976.

Hersey, Frank W. E., <u>Heroes of the Battle Road</u>, Perry Walton, Boston, 1930.

Hudson, Alfred S., <u>The History of Sudbury, Massachusetts, 1638-1889</u>, The Town of Sudbury, 1889.

Hudson, Charles, <u>History of the Town of Lexington</u>, Houghton Mifflin Co., Boston, 1913.

Hudson, Frederic, <u>Harper's New Monthly Magazine</u>, No. 300, May 1875, Vol. L., "The Concord Fight," Harper and Brothers, New York, 1875.

Hurd, Hamilton, <u>History of Middlesex County Massachusetts, Vol. I</u>, J. W. Lewis and Co., Philadelphia, 1890.

King, Daniel P., <u>Address Commemorative of Seven Young Men of Danvers Who Were Slain in the Battle of Lexington</u>, Salem, 1835.

Lathram, R. J. W., <u>British Military Bayonets from 1700 to 1945</u>, London, 1967.

Lindsay, Merrill, <u>The New England Gun</u>, David McKay Co., New York, 1975.

Moore, Warren, Weapons of the American Revolution and Accoutrements, Promontory Press, New York, 1967.

Muller, John, A Treatise of Artillery 1780, Museum Restoration Service, Bloomfield, Ontario.

Newman, George C., The History of Weapons of the American Revolution, Bonanza Books, New York, 1967.

Peterson, Harold L., Arms and Armor in Colonial America, 1526 - 1783, New York, Bramhall House, 1956.

Phalen, Harold R., History of the Town of Acton, Middlesex Printing Co., Cambridge, 1954.

Phillips, James Duncan, Salem in the Eighteenth Century, Essex Institute, Salem, 1969.

Quarles, Benjamin, The Negro and the American Revolution, The University of North Carolina Press, Chapel Hill, 1961.

Reynolds, Grindall, A Collection of Historical and Other Papers, University Press, Cambridge, 1896.

Sewall, Samuel, The History of Woburn, Wiggin and Lunt, Boston, 1868.

Shattuck, Lemuel, A History of the Town of Concord, Russell, Odiorne and Co., Concord, 1835.

Shy, John, Toward Lexington: The Role of the British Army in the Coming of the American Revolution, Princeton, 1965.

Stowe, Hambrick, C. E. and Donna D. Smerlas, Massachusetts Militia Companies and Officers in the Lexington Alarm, New England Historic Genealogical Society, Boston, 1976.

Summer, William H., A History of East Boston with Biographical Sketches, J. E. Tilton and Co., Boston, 1858.

Tapley, Harriett Silvester, Chronicles of Danvers (Old Salem Village) 1632-1923, The Danvers Historical Society, Danvers, Mass., 1923.

Temple, Josiah K., History of Framingham, Massachusetts, Framingham, 1887.

Tolman, George, Events of April Nineteen, Concord Antiquarian Society, Concord, Mass.

Tourtellot, Arthur B., Lexington and Concord, Doubleday, New York, 1959.

Trask, Richard B., Danvers Gazette, Vol. I, No. I, Danvers Bicentennial Committee, Danvers, Mass., 1975.

Webster, Donald B., American Socket Bayonets 1717-1873, Museum Restoration Service, Ottawa, 1964.

Wheeler, Ruth R., Concord Climate for Freedom, Concord Antiquarian Society, Concord, Mass., 1967.

CONGRESSIONAL REPORTS

Final Report of the Boston National Historic Sites Commission to the Congress of the United States, June 16, 1960.

The Lexington-Concord Battle Road: Interim Report of the Boston National Historic Sites Commission to the Congress of the United States, June 16, 1958.

NATIONAL PARK SERVICE REPORTS

Abel, L. J. and Cordelia T. Snow, The Excavation of Sites 22 and 23, Minute Man National Historical Park, Massachusetts, National Park Service, 1966.

Kryston, Cynthia E., The Muster Field: Historic Data, Minute Man National Historic Site, National Park Service, Concord, Mass., 1972.

Luzader, John F., Elisha Jones or "Bullet Hole House," Minute Man National Historical Park, Historic Structures Report Part II, National Park Service, 1968.

Luzader, John F., Samuel Hartwell House and Ephraim Hartwell Tavern, Minute Man National Historical Park, Historic Structures Report, Part 1, National Park Service, 1968.

Malcolm, Joyce Lee, The Scene of the Battle, 1775, Historic Grounds Report, Minute Man National Historical Park, National Park Service, 1985.

Ronsheim, Robert D., Troop Movement Map, Narrative Section, Minute Man National Historical Park, National Park Service, 1964.

Snow, David H., Archeological Research Report, Excavation at Site 264 The Thomas Nelson, Jr. House, Minute Man National Historical Park, National Park Service, 1973.

10148897R0

Made in the USA
Lexington, KY
28 June 2011